Jonathan
Goforth

MEN OF FAITH

Jonathan Goforth

Rosalind Goforth

BETHANY HOUSE PUBLISHERS
MINNEAPOLIS, MINNESOTA 55438
A Division of Bethany Fellowship, Inc.

The original edition, *Goforth of China,* was first published and copyrighted by Zondervan Publishing House in 1937. The edited version, *Jonathan Goforth,* is printed by special arrangement.

Jonathan Goforth
Rosalind Goforth

Library of Congress Catalog Card Number 85–73425

ISBN 0–87123–842–X
Copyright © 1986

Published by Bethany House Publishers
A Division of Bethany Fellowship, Inc.
6820 Auto Club Road, Minneapolis, Minnesota 55438

Printed in the United States of America

CONTENTS

INTRODUCTION

Many details in this record can be better understood after knowing something of the author, who for forty-nine years was Jonathan Goforth's closest companion and the mother of his eleven children.

I was born near Kensington Gardens, London, England, on May 6, 1864, coming to Montreal, Canada with my parents three years later. From my earliest childhood, much time was spent beside the easel of my artist-father, who thought that I should be an artist. My education, apart from art, was received chiefly in private schools or from my own mother. In May, 1885, I graduated from the Toronto School of Art and began preparations to leave in the autumn for London to complete my art studies.

When I was twelve years old, I heard Mr. Alfred Sandham speak on John 3:16 at a revival meeting. As he fervently presented the love of God, I yielded myself absolutely to the Lord Jesus and stood up among others, publicly confessing Him as my Master. On the way home from that meeting, I was told again and again how foolish it was for me to think I could be sure Christ had received

me. So early the next morning, I got my Bible, and turning the pages over and over, I prayed that I might get
some word which would assure me Christ had really received me. At last I came to John 6:37, "Him that cometh
to me I will in no wise cast out."

Then I was told I was too young to be received, and
again I went to my Bible. I came, after searching a long
time, to these words, "Those that seek me early shall find
me" (Prov. 8:17). I have never doubted since then that I
was the Lord's child.

When I was nineteen I began to pray that if the Lord
wanted me to marry, He would lead to me one *wholly
given up to Him and to His service.* I wanted no other.
One Sunday in June, of that year, a stranger took the
place of our Bible-class teacher. He was introduced to
me, the organist, as Mr. Henry O'Brien. Three days later,
two large parties were crossing the lake on the same boat,
one, an artists' picnic, bound for the Niagara Falls, the
other, bound for the Niagara-on-the-Lake Bible Conference. I was with the former group, but my heart was with
the others. That evening, both groups returning on the
same boat, I was sitting in the artist circle beside my
brother when Mr. O'Brien touched me, saying, "Why,
you are my organist of Sunday last! You are the very one
I want to join us in the Mission next Saturday. We are to
have a workers' meeting and tea, and I would like you to
meet them all." I was on the point of saying this was
impossible when my brother whispered, "You have no
time. You are going to England." Partly to show him I
could do as I pleased, I said to Mr. O'Brien, "Very well;
expect me on Saturday."

As Mr. O'Brien turned to leave, he called to a very
shabby fellow whom he introduced as "Jonathan Goforth,
our city missionary." I forgot the shabbiness of his clothes
however, for the wonderful challenge in his eyes!

The following Saturday found me in the large, square

workers' room of the Toronto Mission Union. Just as the meeting was about to begin, Jonathan Goforth was called out of the room. As he rose, he placed his Bible on the chair. Something happened then which I could never explain, nor try to excuse. Suddenly, I stepped past four or five people, took up his Bible and returned to my seat. Rapidly I turned the leaves and found the book worn almost to shreds in parts and marked from cover to cover. I quickly returned it to the chair, and returning to my seat, I tried to look very innocent. As I sat there, I said to myself, *"That is the man I would like to marry!"*

That very day, I was chosen as one of a committee with Jonathan Goforth to open a new mission. In the weeks that followed, I had many opportunities to glimpse his inner greatness. So when, in that autumn he asked, "Will you join your life with mine for China?" my answer was, "Yes," without a moment's hesitation. But a few days later he said, "Will you give me your promise that *always* you will allow me to put my Lord and His work first, even before you?" I gave an inward gasp before replying, "Yes, I will, *always*," for was not this the very kind of man I had prayed for?

A few days after my promise was given, the first test in keeping it came. I had been indulging in dreams of the beautiful engagement ring that was soon to be mine. Then Jonathan came to me and said, "You will not mind, will you, if I do not get an engagement ring?" He went on to tell with great enthusiasm of his distribution of books and pamphlets on China from his room in Knox College. Every cent was needed for this important work. This was my first lesson in *real values*.

By the end of the next two years, which were given to the work in the East End slums, art had practically dropped out of my life. In its place had come a deep desire to be a worthy life-partner of one so wholly yielded to his Divine Master, as I knew Jonathan Goforth to be.

Mrs. Rosalind Goforth

1

EARLY LEADINGS

Even a child is known by his doings.
                                        Proverbs 10:11

While the Goforths were attending a summer conference, south of Chicago, the chairman introduced our
"brilliant speaker" with overflowing praise. The stranger
had been sitting with head bowed and face hidden. As
he stepped forward he stood a moment as if in prayer,
then said:

"Friends, when I listen to such words as we have just
been hearing I have to remind myself of the woodpecker
story: A certain woodpecker flew up to the top of a high
pine tree and gave three hard pecks on the side of the
tree as woodpeckers are wont to do. At that instant a bolt
of lightning struck the tree leaving it a heap of splinters
on the ground. The woodpecker had flown to a tree nearby
where it clung in terror and amazement at what had taken
place. There it hung expecting more to follow, but as all
remained quiet it began to chuckle to itself saying, 'Well,
well, well! Who would have imagined that just three pecks
of my beak could have such power as that!' "

When the laughter ceased the speaker went on, "Yes, friends, remember, if you or I take glory to ourselves which belongs only to Almighty God, we are not only as foolish as this woodpecker, but we commit a very grievous sin, for the Lord hath said, 'My glory will I not give to another.'"

Many times Jonathan Goforth on returning from a meeting would greet his wife with, "Well, I've had to remind myself of the woodpecker tonight."

Early in life he chose as his motto, "Not by might nor by power, but by my spirit" (Zech. 4:6).

Jonathan Goforth was always God's radiant servant. Of all the messages which reached his wife after he had entered the gloryland, none touched her more than the following: A poor servant girl, on hearing of his passing said to her master, "When Dr. Goforth has been here I have often watched his face and have wondered *if God looked like him!*" That dear girl saw in his sightless face what she hoped for in her Heavenly Father!

John Goforth came to western Ontario, Canada, from Yorkshire, England, as one of the early pioneers in 1840. His wife dead, he brought with him his three sons, John, Simeon, and Francis. Francis married a young woman, named Jane Bates, from Northern Ireland and settled on a farm near London, Ontario. Of their family of ten boys and one girl, Jonathan was the seventh child. He was born on his father's farm, near Thorndale, February 10, 1859.

Those were hard, grinding times for both father and mother, and for the boys, who helped out by working at odd jobs with neighboring farmers. Years later Jonathan remarked, "I remember my father telling of his having tramped through the bush all the way from Hamilton to our home near London, a distance of seventy miles, with a sack of flour on his back."

When Jonathan was but five years of age, he had a miraculous escape from death. We quote from his diary:

"My uncle was driving a load of grain to market. I was to be taken to my father's farm some miles distant. The bags were piled high on the wagon, and a place was made for me just behind my uncle in a hole which was deemed perfectly safe. Suddenly while driving down a hill, a front wheel sank deep into a rut, causing the wagon to lurch to one side. I was thrown out of my hole and started to slide down. Before my uncle could reach me I had dropped between the front and back wheels. The back wheel had just reached me, and I felt it crushing against my hip. At that same instant my uncle also reached me, but I was so pinned under the wheel he had difficulty in getting me free. A fraction of an inch farther and my hip would have been crushed."

The above was but the first of many remarkable deliverances from imminent death in Jonathan Goforth's life.

In writing of those early years he said,

"One thing I look back to as a great blessing in my later life, was mother's habit of getting me to read the Psalms to her. I was only five.

"From those earliest years I wanted to be a Christian. When I was seven years of age a lady gave me a fine Bible with brass clasps and marginal references. This was another impetus to search the Scriptures. One Sunday, when ten years old, I was attending church with my mother. It was Communion Sunday, and while she was partaking of the Lord's Supper, I sat alone on one of the side seats. Suddenly it came over me with great force that if God called me away I would not go to heaven. How I wanted to be a Christian! I am sure if someone had spoken to me about my soul's salvation I would have yielded my heart to Christ then."

For almost ten "school" years Jonathan was under the great handicap of being obliged to work on the farm, from

April till October or even November. Dr. Andrew Vining, a Canadian Baptist leader and one of Jonathan's early schoolmates, remembers this time well:

> "My friendship with him began one day when he challenged and very effectively trounced a schoolhouse bully who had been making life unhappy for me, a younger and smaller boy. The years of his matchless service have given significance to one clear recollection I have of him. He had a habit of standing during recess in front of the maps which hung in the schoolroom. I clearly remember seeing him, day after day, studying these maps: the World, Asia, Africa."

At the age of fifteen, Jonathan's father put him in charge of their second farm, called "The Thamesford Farm," some twenty miles distant from the home farm. Jonathan wrote:

> "I was ambitious to run my farm scientifically, and I was well rewarded for my pains for my butter always sold for the highest price in the London market. In farming and cultivating I consistently endeavoured to apply scientific methods and with gratifying results. In handing over the farm, Father had called special attention to one very large field which had become choked with weeds. Father said, 'Get that field clear and ready for seeding. At harvest time I'll return and inspect.' "

Jonathan, in later years, kept many an audience spellbound as he described the labor he put into that field. Ploughing and reploughing, sunning the deadly roots and ploughing again till the whole field was ready for seeding; then how he procured the very best seed for sowing, and finally, he would tell of that summer morning, when just at harvest-time, his father arrived, and how his heart thrilled with joy as he led his father to a high place from which the whole field of beautiful waving grain could be seen. He spoke not a word—only waited for the coveted "well done." His father stood for several moments silently examining the field for a sign of a weed but there was none. Turning to his son he just smiled. "That smile was all the reward I wanted," Goforth would say. "I knew my father was pleased. So will it be if we are faithful to the trust our Heavenly Father gives us."

About this time an incident occurred which might well have ended fatally for the young lad. He was assisting at a neighbor's barn-raising, an affair sufficiently dangerous to keep the womenfolk in suspense till all was over. Operations had reached the dangerous point when the heavy beams had one by one been hauled up and laid on the cross "bent." Jonathan was standing below these beams in the center of the barn when a sudden cry rang out, "Take care, the bent is giving!" Looking up, he saw the beams had already started downward. There was not time to escape by running. There was but one thing to do— stand still and watch the beams as they fell and dodge between two. This he did, escaping unhurt. Here again, God delivered Jonathan from certain death.

While on the Thamesford Farm he became ambitious to study law and become a politician. After the evening chores were done he would walk miles to attend a political meeting. At the back of the home was a swamp. Here he would get out alone and practice speaking. Travellers on the highway some distance away could hear his voice.

After finishing a short commercial course in London, Ontario, seventeen-year-old Goforth returned to the country school near his home, to struggle through his high school there. The Rev. Lachlan Cameron, a Presbyterian, visited the school regularly, holding Bible-study services with the pupils.

Jonathan's marked proficiency in art penmanship, much in vogue at that time, attracted Mr. Cameron's attention. The lad, always responsive to kindness, took a great liking for the minister and determined to hear him in his own pulpit. One who was present at that first Sunday gives the following:

"Almost sixty years have passed since then but I can still see the young stranger sitting immediately in front of the minister with an eager, glowing look on his face and listening with great intentness to every word of the sermon."

It was Mr. Cameron's unvarying custom to close each sermon with a direct appeal for decisions. We give in Jonathan's own words what took place his third Sunday under Mr. Cameron:

"Mr. Cameron seemed to look right at me as he pled, during his sermon, for all who had not, to accept the Lord Jesus Christ. His words cut me deeply and I said to myself, 'I must decide before he is through.' But contrary to his usual custom, he suddenly stopped and began to pray. During the prayer the devil whispered, 'Put off your decision for another week.' Then immediately after the prayer, Mr. Cameron leaned over the pulpit and with great intensity and fervor again pled for decisions. As I sat there, without any outward sign except to simply bow my head, I yielded myself up to Christ."

At the next Communion, Jonathan joined the church and at once began to seek avenues of service for his new-found Master. He was given a Sunday-school class but this did not satisfy him. He sent off for tracts and became an object of wonder to the staid old elders, and amusement to the young, as he stood Sunday after Sunday at the church door giving to each one a tract! Very soon he started a Sunday evening service in the old schoolhouse a mile or more from his home.

We give two stories of this time in his own words:

"At the time of my conversion I was living with my brother Will. Our parents came on a visit, and stayed a month or so. For some time I felt the Lord would have me lead family worship. So one night I said, 'We will have worship tonight, so please don't scatter after supper.' I was afraid of what my father would say for we

had not been accustomed to saying 'grace' before meals
much less having family worship.

"I read a chapter in Isaiah and after a few comments
we all knelt in prayer. Much to my relief, father never
said a word. Family worship continued as long as I was
home. Some months later my father took a stand for
Jesus Christ."

The following occurred while he was attending high
school in Ingersoll, twelve miles from the home farm:

"My teacher was an ardent follower of Tom Paine.
He persuaded all the boys in our class to his way of
thinking. The jeers and arguments of my classmates
proved too much for me. Suddenly all the foundations
slipped. I was confounded! Instead of going to my minister or any other human aid, I felt constrained to take
the Word of God alone as my guide. Night and day for
a considerable period ot time, I did little else than search
the Scriptures until, finally, I was so solidly grounded
I have never had a shadow of a doubt since. All my
classmates, as well as our teacher, were brought back
from infidelity, the teacher becoming one of my lifelong
friends."

For one year he still retained his ambition of becoming a lawyer and a *good* politician, believing he should
serve the Lord in this way. His Master, however, had
other plans for this servant.

One Saturday afternoon Jonathan had occasion to go
with horse and buggy to see his brother Will, whose farm
was some fifteen miles away. As he was leaving early
Sunday morning, Will's father-in-law handed Jonathan a
well-worn copy of *The Memoirs of Robert Murray
M'Cheyne*, saying, "Read this, my boy, it'll do you good."

The day was one of those balmy, Indian Summer days
in October. Jonathan had not gone far when remember-
ing the book he opened it and began to read as he drove
slowly on. From the first page the message of the book
gripped him. Coming to a clump of trees by the roadside,

he stopped the horse, and tethering it to a tree made a
comfortable seat of dried leaves and gave himself up to
the *Memoirs*. Not till the shadows had lengthened did he
realize how much time had passed.

The thrilling story of M'Cheyne's spiritual struggles
and victories, and his life-sacrifices for the salvation of
the Jews, had sunk deep into his soul. He rose and continued his journey, but in those quiet hours by the roadside, Jonathan Goforth had caught the vision and had
made the decision which changed the whole course of his
life. He resolved to give his life to leading unsaved souls
to the Savior.

At once arrangements were made for the young man
to come regularly to Rev. Cameron's for lessons in Latin
and Greek in preparation for his entering Knox College.
And for two years previously to his entering Knox College, Toronto, he rose two hours earlier each morning in
order to get time for unbroken Bible study, before getting
to work or off to school.

The story of Jonathan Goforth's call to foreign service
we now give in his own words:

"Although I was clearly led to be a minister of the
gospel, I rejected all thought of being a foreign missionary. All my thoughts and plans were for work in
Canada. While attending high school in Ingersoll . . .
I heard that Dr. G. L. Mackay, of Formosa, was to speak
in Knox Church, Ingersoll. A schoolmate persuaded me
to go with him to the meeting. Dr. Mackay, in his vivid
manner, pressed home the needs and claims of Formosa
upon us. Among other things, he said, 'For two years I
have been going up and down Canada trying to persuade some young man to come over to Formosa and
help me, but in vain. It seems that no one has caught
the vision. I am therefore going back alone. It will not
be long before my bones will be lying on some For-
mosan hillside. To me the heartbreak is that no young
man has heard the call to come and carry on the work
that I have begun.'

"As I listened to these words, I was overwhelmed
with shame. Had the floor opened up and swallowed
me out of sight, it would have been a relief. . . . I heard
the Lord's voice saying, 'Who will go for us and whom
shall we send?' And I answered, 'Here am I; send me.'
From that hour I became a foreign missionary. I eagerly
read everything I could find on foreign missions and set
to work to get others to catch the vision I had caught
of the claims of the unreached, unevangelized millions
on earth."

At last the time drew near for Jonathan Goforth to
leave the old farm home for the new, untried city life at
Knox College. His mother, noted among the neighbors
for her fine needlecraft, worked far into the night putting
her best effort into finishing clothes for the dear boy who
was to be the scholar of the family.

During the last days at home Jonathan's heart was
thrilled as he thought how soon he was to live and work
with other young men who, like himself, had given themselves to the most sacred, holy calling of winning men to
Christ. He had visions of prayer meetings and Bible study
groups on reaching Knox where, in company with kindred
spirits, he could dig deeper into his beloved Bible. His
joyous, optimistic spirit had reached fever heat when he
arrived in Toronto and entered Knox College.

2

BEGINNING AT JERUSALEM

*When he found his own soul needed Jesus Christ,
it became a passion with him to take Jesus Christ
to every soul.*

Said of Jonathan Goforth

On entering Knox College, Jonathan Goforth quite unconsciously carried the city-despised earmarks of the country. He was unconventional to a degree, and utterly unacquainted with city habits and ways.

He had been but a very few days in his new environment when he became keenly conscious that his home-made garments would not measure up in the college. He was very poor, depending entirely on his own resources, for he would not look to his father for help. With a desire to economize as much as possible, he bought a quantity of material, intending to take it to a city seamstress to make into a new outfit. But before he could do so, the students got wind of it. Late that night a number of students came into his room, secured their victim and cut a hole at one end of the material. They put his head through it and made him run up and down the corridor through a barrage of hilarious students.

That night he knelt with his Bible before him and struggled through the greatest humiliation and the first disappointment of his life. The dreams he had been indulging in but a few days before had vanished, and before him, for a time at least, lay *a lone road*.

The character which God was forging into Jonathan's life is illuminated by Dr. Charles W. Gordon, a classmate of Jonathan Goforth's, who wrote the following letter soon after Jonathan's death.

". . . It was during my college days, of course, that I first came to know him. . . .

"Jonathan Goforth in his enthusiastic innocence, aroused the amusement of his tablemates at dinner with his naive stories of his experiences in the Ward [a slum]. . . . He was too innocent to recognize a harlot when he saw her, or too pitiful to avoid her. His dinner-table tales sometimes amused, at other times annoyed, his fellow students. His activities in the saving of the lost aroused in some a contempt for his simplicity. He became a subject for an 'Initiation Ceremony'; hailed at midnight before his judges, students of Knox College, he was subjected, I learned, to indignities, and warned against further breaches of good form by his tales of his 'experiences with sinners.' Goforth was deeply hurt, not so much for himself, but that such a thing should happen in a 'Christian college'. . . .

"The day came when honored by the whole body of students, he went forth to his mission to China, their representative supported by their contributions, and backed by their prayers, the first Canadian missionary to be supported in his work by his fellow-students. . . .

"Twenty-two, I think, were members of our graduating class; the great majority of them volunteered for service in the mission field at home or abroad. Not one of them, I am quite sure but would greatly love Jonathan Goforth and thank God for his influence on their characters and lives. . . ."

Without one exception, every student who had taken part in what had hurt and humiliated him during those early days at Knox, had, before he left the College, come to him expressing their regret.

On his very first day in Toronto, Jonathan Goforth walked down through the slum-ward, south of the college, praying that God would open the way for him to enter those needy homes with the gospel of Jesus Christ. The first Sunday morning was spent in visiting the Don jail, a practice he kept up throughout his whole college course. Until the warden came to know him, he was allowed only into the assembly hall. Then, when he had won the official's confidence, he was given liberty to go into the corridors.

One Sunday morning, as he was standing in the center of the corridor, about to begin his address, a man burst out in a bombastic manner, "I don't believe there is a God." There was tense silence for a moment. Then Jonathan walked over to the man's cell, and said in a very friendly way, "Why, my good friend, this Book I have here speaks about you." The man laughed incredulously. What could any book have to say about him? Goforth turned to Psalm 14, and read the first verse: "The fool hath said in his heart, There is no God." At that the whole corridor burst out laughing. Although he had intended to speak on another subject, he went ahead and spoke from the text just quoted. The men paid close attention, and when he was through, some were in tears. He then went from cell to cell, making a personal appeal to each man. Several made definite stands for Christ that morning.

For two years his work in the slums was in connection with the William Street Mission. Then he became city missionary for the Toronto Mission Union, a faith mission which guaranteed him no stated salary. Sometimes he didn't have enough even to buy a postage stamp. The four years of Goforth's life as city missionary of the Toronto Mission Union gave him many opportunities to prove God's faithfulness in answering prayer for physical needs. We give one instance along this line.

When graduation time drew near, Goforth began to feel the urgent need for a good suit. He prayed very definitely for this. One day, while walking down Yonge Street, the head of a well-known tailoring establishment, Mr. Berkinshaw, was standing in front of his shop and on seeing Goforth, he hailed him with, "Say, Goforth, you're the very man I'm looking for! Come in." A black suit of the finest quality was brought out. Goforth objected, saying, "I do need a suit, but this is too much for my pocket." Mr. Berkinshaw, however, insisted he try on the suit. It fitted perfectly. "Now," said the tailor, "are you too proud to accept it as a gift? For it's yours for the taking. A customer of mine had the suit made but it didn't please him, so it was left on my hands." On each furlough, Goforth always dealt with that firm "as a debt of honor."

As I write, an interesting word-picture of those student days at Knox College comes from an old elder in Toronto who, for many years, had been Jonathan Goforth's prayer-helper:

"On one occasion, Goforth was scheduled to speak at a certain place on Sunday. When about to leave for the station he found he had only sufficient money to buy a ticket one station short of where he was to speak. At once he decided to get his ticket to that station and walk the rest of the way, a distance of ten miles. This he did. When about eight miles of his foot-journey had been covered he came upon a group of road-menders sitting by the roadside. Glad to rest he sat down among them. One offered him a "pull" from his whiskey flask! It was not long before he had the ears and hearts of his audience. On leaving he gave all a hearty invitation to his meeting the following day. To his great joy several of the men turned up. And at least one of these men decided for Christ that day."

On weekdays, Jonathan spent much of his time visiting in the slum district. His strategy was to knock at a door, and when it opened a few inches, he would put his foot in the crack. He would then tell them his business and if, as was usually the case, they said they were not interested and went to close the door, his foot prevented them. As he persisted, the people of the house almost invariably gave way and let him in. Of all the many hundreds of homes that he visited during his years of slum-work, there were only two where he failed to gain an entrance.

He carried his message into all kinds of places, even brothels, visiting seventeen of these places on one street. It was his joy to be able to lead a number of the young women to Christ.

One night as he was coming out from a street that had a particularly evil reputation, a policeman friend of his met him. "How have you the courage to go into those places?" he asked. "*We* never go except in twos or threes." "Well, *I* never go alone, either," Goforth answered. "There is always Someone with me."

Goforth was returning to the college late one other night, from some ministry in the slum ward, when he noticed a light in a basement window. Always keen, not only to take advantage of opportunities but to make them, he tried the door beside the window and finding it unlocked, walked in to face a group of gamblers. One of them asked his name. "Goforth," he replied. This so amused the men, they broke into hearty laughter. Cards were pushed aside and Jonathan was given a chance to preach Christ from his ever ready Bible.

The experience which he had had in the slums of Toronto proved invaluable to Jonathan Goforth in after years, for he found Chinese human nature very much the same as Canadian human nature.

Goforth's first Home Mission field lay in the Muskoka district. He had four preaching points, Allensville, Port Sydney, Brunel, and Huntsville. The field was twenty-two miles long and twelve miles wide. He set out at once to visit every home in the whole area, regardless of denomination or creed, and this, so far as he knew, he succeeded in doing. One of the Huntsville church leaders reckoned that Goforth walked at least sixteen miles each Sunday, besides speaking three times.

At Allensville, Port Sydney, and Brunel, Goforth's work soon began to show very encouraging results. The little frame buildings in which the services were held became too small to hold the people, many of whom had to walk miles to get to church. The people would be crowded in everywhere, even on the pulpit steps. Once, in his excitement, he flung his hand back and hit several people behind him, thus causing convulsions in the audience. A number of people, notably Tom Howard, one of the most notorious characters in the countryside, were led to Christ. This man broke right down in the middle of a service and confessed his sins. When Goforth discovered Howard had a fine voice, he appointed him to lead the singing. He would almost "raise the roof" with his intensity, the tears streaming down his cheeks.

How to reach the boys of Huntsville was from the beginning a problem for the young missionary. He could not persuade them to come to church, though he asked them often enough. One afternoon as the boys were playing baseball on the common across the river from the church, Goforth joined them. After a while the profanity became so bad, he dropped his bat and excused himself from the game. The boys were thereupon most apologetic and promised they would not offend again. After the game, the boys accompanied Goforth to the church where they spent an hour studying the Bible together. This continued almost every evening throughout the summer.

On one occasion while following the trail through a thick bush, as he turned a sharp bend in the path he came face to face with a great bear just to one side of the path. The bear rose, sat back on its haunches, and stared. For brief moments, Goforth stood still and stared back at the bear. Then he thought, "I'm on my Master's business and He can keep me." Going steadily but slowly forward, he had to almost touch the bear to pass him but the great beast made no sign of moving.

After Goforth's death, Mr. Collier, head of the Yonge Street tailoring firm, summarized Jonathan's ministry thus:

> "His true and simple faith in God was passed on to others. As his Master, he went about doing good. Jonathan Goforth is dead so far as this world is concerned, but he is not dead, his spirit lives on not only in the 'better world' but in the lives of those whom he has touched here. We will never know how far-reaching his ministry has gone—it will go on and on, forever. . . . I and others have lost a wonderful friend. I loved to have him come in and always felt that I had met a good man who influenced my life."

3

THE VISION GLORIOUS!

Obedience is the one qualification for further vision.

G. Campbell Morgan

Jonathan Goforth's heart was on fire for foreign missions. He was sent out one Sunday to fill a pulpit, and as usual, spoke on missions. On Monday morning, as the train was pulling out of the station, a man asked if he might share his seat. "I heard you preach in our church yesterday," said the man. "When I heard that you were coming to speak on missions, I prepared myself with five cents for the collection. I usually give coppers on Sunday, but seeing that this particular collection was to go for missions, I decided that I couldn't think of giving less than five cents. After you commenced speaking, I began to wish it were ten cents. A little later, and I thought a quarter too little. You were not half-way through till I wished I had a dollar bill, and by the time you finished, I would gladly have given a five-dollar bill."

Some months later, Goforth received a letter from this man's pastor saying, "I suppose you will remember having had a conversation with a certain member of my congregation on the train. Well, that man has since sold a piece of property and has given several hundred dollars of the proceeds to foreign missions."

The time came when Jonathan Goforth faced the problem of how he was to get to China. His own church had no work in that country. So, he applied to the China Inland Mission.

But when his fellow-students at Knox College learned of his plans, they decided to raise the necessary funds and start a mission in China with Jonathan Goforth as their missionary.

This decision came in the midst of a movement at Knox that was coincident with a revival of missionary interest throughout a large part of the Christian world. At the East Northfield Conference in 1886, the Student Volunteer Movement was set in motion. On the last day at Northfield one hundred young men and women announced their willingness to become missionaries. The movement spread in a truly amazing fashion through the universities and theological schools of the continent. President McCosh of Princeton said that "not since Pentecost had there been such an offering of young lives."

At Knox and in other Canadian Colleges, daily prayer-meetings for missions were started. In the winter of 1886–87, among the students of Knox and Queen's alone, there were thirty-three volunteers for the foreign field.

The Knox students felt it was necessary to secure the cooperation of the College Alumni in sending Goforth. The matter was brought up at the annual meeting of the Alumni Association, in the fall of 1886. Many of the Alumni were strongly set against the scheme, arguing that the Presbyterian Church had too many fields already. It was also urged that her Home Mission work came first, and was all that she could handle. One man after another spoke with such telling force against the scheme, that its

promoters feared the battle was lost. Then Jonathan Goforth was called upon. For him the issue was crystal clear.
He reminded them of Joshua going down to the rim of
the swollen floods of Jordan in obedience to God's command. He did not wait for a bridge to be thrown across,
but went forward by faith and the way opened up. "As
soon as we are prepared to go forward and preach the
Gospel at God's command," he went on, "then the Lord
of the harvest will surely supply the need." When he had
finished speaking, the Alumni Association, without any
further discussion, voted unanimously to support the
venture.

The Alumni of Knox College had been won over. The
next step was to win the official sanction of the Church.
Jonathan Goforth had already done much on his own
account to turn the mind of the Church toward China.
He had bought hundreds of copies of Hudson Taylor's
China's Spiritual Need and Claims, mailing them chiefly
to ministers. The expense of this undertaking was first
shouldered by himself. Then, later, gifts came in which
enabled him to carry it on. One who knew him at this
time tells of frequently going to his room to help in mailing out the books. In the room were piles of books and
pamphlets on China ready to be sent out. Sometimes,
three or four students were helping. A regular routine
was observed, Goforth first reading aloud letters received
containing donations for the work, many of these being
small gifts from Sunday-school children who had heard
him speak. Then all knelt in prayer for blessing on the
books sent out, and thanksgiving for gifts received.

We cannot doubt but this work was an important
agency in forwarding and feeding the remarkable tide of
interest in foreign missions of this period. Dr. Henry W.
Frost, for many years Home Director of the China Inland
Mission for Canada and the United States, writes the
following striking tribute:

"In the year 1885, I attended for the first time, the Believers' Conference held at Niagara-on-the-Lake, Ontario. . . . [At this conference] a missionary afternoon was given to Mr. Blackstone and Mr. Goforth for addresses upon foreign missions. I was old enough to be in business at that time, and yet, I had never heard anyone speak on work amongst the heathen. It was largely curiosity, therefore, that took me to the afternoon meeting.

"The first speaker was Mr. Wm. E. Blackstone, who gave us a pyrotechnic display, intellectually speaking, which was illuminating and thrilling and which left us exhilarated as touching divine possibilities. The second speaker was the unknown Jonathan Goforth. The first thing that I discovered about this young man was that he had the face of an angel, and the second thing was— I am tempted to say it—that he had the tongue of an arch-angel. Never had I been so stirred by an address. And, besides, the speaker was not content to depend alone upon his utterances; he had hung on every side back of the platform, charts which appealed to the eye and of these he spoke one by one and with great exactness.

"The chart which impressed me most was the one in the center, and which showed the religious condition of the world's inhabitants. In the lower half of this chart, were nine hundred black squares representing the nine hundred millions of heathendom. In the midst of these black squares was a white dot which set forth the Christian Church in heathendom.

"As Mr. Goforth described these black squares and this one tiny white dot, a great conviction took hold upon me. I felt that the church at home was guilty of a great crime . . . nine hundred millions of people in such midnight spiritual darkness when Christ was the light that lighteneth every man that cometh into the world. Sitting there, looking and listening, I cried in my inmost soul, 'O God, what can I—what shall I do?' . . .

"I could not go; but God gave me a work to do for

China while at home and out of it has come the China
Inland Mission in North America."

Of the children's response to his message, Goforth
himself wrote:

"I spent a Sabbath talking on missions at a certain
place. The Sunday-school boys and girls were greatly
interested. How did I know? Well, when I got through
speaking, a number of them came forward, some with
pennies, some with five-cent pieces and even twenty-
five cent pieces. But the interest didn't end there, for
the next day as I was staying at the manse, they came
in ones and twos and even in groups of eight or ten with
their offerings for missions. On Monday forenoon, as I
was going down the street, I met a crowd of sunny faces
on the way to school and they said, 'We are going to
China too when we grow big.' "

Among Jonathan Goforth's papers we found the following story for children which will speak for itself:

"I remember once, when I was but a little boy,
someone gave me five cents. I never had so much money
before. I felt rich. I thought, 'Why, these five cents will
buy six sticks of candy!' I raced into the house to ask
my mother if I might not go to the store at once and
buy that candy. My mother said, 'No, you may not go
for it is Saturday evening and the sun will soon be setting. You must wait until Monday. I never felt so im-
patient about Sunday before. It came between me and
the candy. Just then something seemed to say to me,
'Well, little boy, do you not think that you ought to give
your five cents to the heathen?' At that time I didn't
know who put that thought into my heart, but I had
heard about a collection for missions announced to be
taken on the morrow and I know now that God's Spirit
spoke to me then. He wanted to make me a missionary
but I wasn't willing. The heathen were far away. I didn't
know much about them and didn't care. But I knew all
about candy and it was only two miles away at the store.
I was very fond of it and decided I must have it. But

that didn't end the struggle. It was candy and the heathen and heathen and the candy contending for that five cents. Finally I went to bed, but couldn't sleep. Usually as soon as my head touched the pillow I was off to sleep, but that night I couldn't get to sleep because of the war going on between the heathen and candy, or between love and selfishness. At last the heathen got the better of it and I decided to go up to Sunday-school next day and put my five cents into the collection. I felt very happy then and in a moment was asleep. But when I awoke the sun had arisen and my selfishness had returned. I wanted the candy and the fight went on, but before Sunday-school time, love had gained a final victory and I went to Sunday-school and when the plate was passed around for the mission collection, I dropped my five cents in. And would you believe me, I felt more happy than if I had got a whole store full of candy!

We are also indebted to Miss Mabeth Standen for the following letter:

"How well I remember the farewell meeting in our old church at Minesing just before Dr. and Mrs. Goforth left for China in 1888. . . .

"As Dr. Goforth closed his address he used an illustration that I never forgot. Referring to the miracle of the feeding of the five thousand, he pictured the disciples taking the bread and fish to the first few rows of the waiting and hungry multitude. Then he imagined these same disciples, instead of going on to the back rows, returning to those who had been already fed and offering them bread and fish until they turned away from it, while the back rows were still starving.

"Said Dr. Goforth, 'What would Christ have thought of His disciples had they acted in this way, and what does He think of us today as we continue to spend most of our time and money in giving the Bread of Life to those who have heard so often while millions in China are still starving?' God spoke to me that night about *my* responsibility regarding China and I promised Him then that if He opened my way, I would when old enough

go to the 'back rows.' Later on when other claims seemed
insistent and one was tempted to care for the front rows
only, the vision of China's need as I had seen it that
night always came before my eyes. I could not get away
from it and finally said, 'Lord, here am I, send me—to
the back rows.' "

Dr. John Buchanan, of India, sends the following vivid
and somewhat amusing picture of Jonathan Goforth at
this period:

"Jonathan Goforth, though young, was even then,
in 1887, a fearless prophet of Jehovah. I well remember
when he and I were sent to Zion Church, Brantford.
The Convenor for Home Missions, was pastor. Zion
Church at that time gave almost exclusively to Home
Missions. . . . At the very beginning of our service, He-
ber's missionary hymn was announced and read in part,
perhaps as a sort of concession to the visitors,—

> *"From Greenland's icy mountains,*
> *From India's coral strand . . .*
> *Waft, waft ye winds His story,*
> *And you ye waters roll,*
> *Till like a sea of glory*
> *It spreads from pole to pole."*

but before the organ could sound, Jonathan Goforth, in
his short homespun, much used brown coat, the sleeves
wrinkled up till too short for his Elijah arms, was on
his feet. In his left hand was the Church Blue Book,
opened at the point where the Zion Church statistics
were revealed; his prophetic eyes flashed; his right con-
demning forefinger pointed at the givings for foreign
missions by Zion Church for the previous year.

" 'No!' he demanded, 'a congregation strong as Zion
Church giving only seventy-eight cents per member a
year for foreign missions, cannot sing such a hymn as
that. *We must sing a penitential Psalm—the 51st.*' The
Psalm was sung with deep emotion. . . ."

Thus all opposition melted away before the enthusi-

asm of these missionary-minded students. The missionary vision captured the Presbyterian Church of Canada
as it never had before. Churches, which formerly had
hardly given a thought to the foreign field, made themselves responsible for the support of missionaries. At the
General Assembly in June of 1887, Jonathan Goforth and
Dr. J. Fraser Smith were appointed to China. In the
following October, Goforth was ordained, and on the
twenty-fifth of the same month, was married to Florence
Rosalind Bell-Smith.

After Goforth's ordination, the Foreign Mission Board
planned for him to go through the churches giving his
addresses on foreign missions until Dr. Smith was through
his course, that the two might go together to China. But
early in January of 1888, reports of a great famine raging
in China caused the Board to hasten Goforth's departure
so that he might carry with him considerable funds which
had been raised for famine relief.

Of that wonderful farewell meeting, words fail one to
describe. On January 19, 1888, the old, historic Knox
Church was filled to capacity. One particularly memor-
able story was told there of a young couple bidding farewell to their home church as they were about to leave for
an African field known as "The White Man's Grave." The
husband said, "My wife and I have a strange dread in
going. We feel much as if we were going down into a pit.
We are willing to take the risk and to go if you, our home
circle, will promise *to hold the ropes.*" One and all promised.

Less than two years passed when the wife and the
little one God had given them succumbed to the dreaded
fever. Soon the husband realized his days too were numbered. Not waiting to send word home of his coming, he
started back at once and arrived at the hour of the
Wednesday prayer meeting. He slipped in unnoticed,
taking a back seat. At the close of the meeting he went

forward. An awe came over the people, for death was written on his face. He said:

> "I am your missionary. My wife and child are buried in Africa and I have come home to die. This evening I listened anxiously, as you prayed, for some mention of your missionary to see if you were keeping your promise, but in vain! You prayed for everything connected with yourselves and your home church, but you forgot your missionary. I seen now why I am a failure as a missionary. It is because *you have failed to hold the ropes!*"

Each speaker at that meeting seemed eager to have a share in sending the Goforths off with joyful enthusiasm. The Goforths' train was to leave at midnight from the Old Market station half a mile away. Soon after eleven o'clock, hundreds started for the station.

Toronto probably never witnessed such a scene as followed. The station platform became literally packed. Hymn after hymn was sung. As the time drew near to start, Dr. Caven of Knox College bared his head and led in prayer. A few moments later, as the train began to move, a great volume of voices joined in singing *Onward Christian Soldiers*—hands were stretched out for a last clasp—then darkness. As the last glimpse of the waving friends vanished, Goforth turned to his wife and bowing his head prayed that they might live worthy of such confidence. Jonathan Goforth's new life had begun, and, incidentally, his training of Rosalind!

4

FOR CHRIST AND CHINA

I gave up all for Christ, and what have I found?
I have found everything in Christ!

John Calvin

On reaching Vancouver, they found the city little more than a heap of charred ruins. Only a short time before it had been swept by a devastating fire. To their unsophisticated eyes, their boat, the S. S. "Parthia" seemed "quite splendid," and it was with the utmost joy and hopefulness they began settling in their cabin.

The following is taken from a letter written by Goforth dated Vancouver, February 4, 1888:

". . . We went on deck at 7 o'clock this morning and watched the ship loosed from her moorings. We had not the slightest wish to stay though strong emotion filled us at thought of leaving "native land,"—more properly, those of you our friends who made Canada a dear spot to us. I never saw Mrs. Goforth more happy than now as we turn out into the ocean towards our future home. Let us win ten thousand Chinese souls. It will please him, our Lord." (How fully was this fulfilled in the years to come!)

The remembrance of the fourteen days that followed ever remained—to Mrs. Goforth—a terrible nightmare! They tried to comfort themselves by the thought that they were only going through what all ocean travellers have to put up with, but the truth finally came out. They discovered that for twenty-five years the "Parthia" had plied the Atlantic. As the years passed, the vessel acquired such a notorious reputation for its rolling, pitching, and heaving that none would take passage on her. So the owners had the boat repainted, renamed the "Parthia" and put on the Pacific run.

Jonathan Goforth's own description of this first journey to China was contained in one sentence. "An ordinary winter voyage; bad enough; sick all the way!"

They landed in China at Shanghai, that great metropolis of the Far East, but the sights which drew many tourists held little attraction for Goforth. He was so wrapped up in his mission that as soon as he and his wife were accommodated in a boarding-house, he at once called on some of the leading missionaries and arranged for a meeting the following day. At this meeting it was decided Goforth should hand over to others the famine funds entrusted to him, for it was thought impossible for him, without the language, to take part himself in famine relief work. It was also decided that the triangular section of country north of the Yellow River, known as North Honan, be given to the Canadian Presbyterian Church as their field.

Before the Goforths left for a town on the northern coast of China for language study, one of the missionaries kindly volunteered to lead them through the great "opium palace" of Shanghai. Palace it truly was! Gorgeously decorated and brilliantly lighted, men and women were stretched on their narrow beds fully dressed, with the opium paraphernalia beside them, none seeming the least ashamed as visitors passed by. Later, Goforth was told that the "far country" of the "Prodigal Son" meant Shanghai to the Chinese. The disgraceful fact that covered every missionary with shame was that these opium palaces and literally streets of brothels lay inside the International Settlement of Shanghai. They were permitted because of the great financial gain derived from them. The governing board of the International Settlement was made up of representatives from so-called Christian countries.

The day after arriving in Chefoo, the Goforths settled in a house offered to them at modest rental by Dr. Williamson, a long-time resident of Chefoo. This home was situated on the outskirts of a village two miles to the east and on the plain below Temple Hill. Within a day or two, Goforth had engaged a teacher and was hard at work on the language and since he, from the first, insisted that the full time for language study must be uninterrupted, getting settled was necessarily slow work.

One day while the Goforths sat at dinner, screams and shouts were heard. Running outside, they found the bedroom at the farther end of the house was on fire. The old, thatched roof, dry as tinder, was ablaze and already beginning to drop fire below. Again and again Goforth ran into the burning rooms. The first things to be rescued were his beloved Bible and a valise containing the money. As he returned for more things his panic-stricken wife grasped the valise and ran for the road, thinking it to be the safest place. In her agitated state she was unconscious of the many eyes eagerly watching for a chance to snatch the valise. Fortunately, Goforth missed it before it was snatched from her. Running to his wife as she stood dazed by the roadside, he said sternly, "Pull yourself together and don't give way to panic! Do you not know the Chinese will steal?" It was the best thing for her for it brought her to her senses and from then on she was quite calm.

It was not a pleasant sight to watch wedding presents,

pictures (one of them of her father painted by himself from a mirror), and other precious *home* things being licked up by the flames, but so it was. Practically everything of real value to them was burned. Later, Goforth tried to comfort his wife by saying, "My dear, do not grieve so. After all, they're *just things*."

The fire meant little more to Goforth than a temporary hindering of his language study, for his optimism remained as unshadowed and his radiant cheerfulness as helpful as if it had not occurred. To his wife, it meant the burning of the bridges behind her as far as art was concerned, and it meant also the dawn of personal responsibility toward the souls of her Chinese sisters.

Just three weeks from the evening they had landed at Chefoo, the Goforths were settling in their second home, a two-story, semi-detached foreign built house within a minute's walk of the seashore.

About the end of April, Goforth gave his wife her first lesson in real giving. Coming to her with his open account book in hand, he said: "I have been going carefully into our accounts and I find we have given a tithe of one year's salary already and we have been married just six months. What would you suggest about it?"

Now his wife had not been accustomed to tithing in her parents' home, and had thought it very generous of her husband to tithe their salary. "If we have already given a tithe of our year's salary, I suppose we need not give any more till the end of the year."

"Do you really feel we should do so?" Jonathan replied gravely, rather taken aback. "To me it seems right when the Lord has done so much for us that we should just close the account to date, and begin again."

This he did. So that year a fifth was given. This was but the first lesson of a "progressive course" in giving, for as the years passed, his wife became accustomed to a half, and on till only sufficient of their income for pressing needs was kept.

Every Sabbath morning found him at the native service on Temple Hill, with notebook and pencil, seeking to get accustomed to the strange sounds of the native language.

The months of July and August seemed constantly interwoven with joy and sorrow. Early in July, a fine young teacher in the C.I.M. Boys' School, named Norris, gave his life in saving his boys from a mad dog. He was bitten in the hand and died a month later. Then, on August 12, Gertrude Goforth arrived bringing with her great joy. For some time the dreaded cholera had been becoming more and more menacing in the native city. One afternoon, a lady from the Baptist Mission called at the Goforths and while returning through the native city, contracted the dreaded cholera and died a few hours later. Late in August, Mrs. Hunter Corbett died suddenly. The Goforths keenly felt her death for she had been like a mother to both of them.

By the middle of August, recruits began to arrive from Canada, among them Dr. and Mrs. J. F. Smith. A little later a cordial letter was received from the most famous of China's missionaries of his day, Rev. Dr. Arthur H. Smith, offering his services as escort on a tour of inspection of North Honan, their future field.

On Sept. 13, 1888, Mr. Goforth and Dr. J. F. Smith started on their exploration tour of North Honan. Of this trip, Goforth records one incident as follows:

"We crossed the northern boundary into Honan province over the Chang River. The country before us lay rich and fertile with villages as thick as farmsteads in most parts of Ontario. To the west could be seen the beautiful Shansi mountains. I was thrilled with the thought of being at last inside our 'Promised Land.' Walking ahead of the carts, I prayed the Lord to give me that section of North Honan as my own field, and as I prayed, I opened "Clark's Scripture Promises," my daily textbook, and found the promise for that day read as follows: *'For as the rain cometh down, and the snow from heaven and watereth the earth and maketh it bring forth and bud, that it may give seed to the sower, and bread to the eater; so shall my word be that goeth forth out of my mouth: it shall not return unto me void, but shall accomplish that which I please, and it shall prosper in the thing whereto I sent it.'* Isaiah 55:10, 11.

"The promise seemed so wonderful, coming as it did just at that juncture, and as I went on, I kept praying that this promise might be fulfilled to that region."

5

WITHIN THE PROMISED LAND

*We are asked to do an impossible task, but we
work with Him who can do the impossible.*
                                        Hudson Taylor

As the Goforth's were preparing to leave Chefoo for
Pangchwang, a village several days' journey nearer North
Honan, a letter arrived from Dr. Hudson Taylor saying:
"Brother, if you would enter that Province, you must *go
forward on your knees.*" These words became the slogan
of the North Honan Mission.

Pangchwang, meaning the village of the Pang family,
was a small village situated a mile or more from the river
bank, in the midst of a thickly populated farming region.
The Goforths found their new home greatly superior to
what they had expected and were able to purchase some
much needed second-hand furniture left for sale by a
missionary then on furlough.

Shortly after Goforth arrived in China, the Rev. Donald McGillivray, his closest friend in Knox College, had
written him that he feared church finances would delay
his coming. Goforth had at once written back, "Come

45

and share with us." But by the time this word had reached
McGillivray, he already was starting for China. Great was
Jonathan's joy when at last his friend reached Pangchwang. It was truly the meeting of David and Jonathan for
them. Their friendship was deep and true and for more
than thirty-five years till Donald McGillivray passed away,
not a shadow darkened their friendship.

McGillivray's progress in the language was phenom-
enal. In one month he memorized all the Chinese characters in John's gospel, being able to give the sound,
tone, and meaning of each character, and this besides the
regular language study. Jonathan Goforth worked just as
hard and just as faithfully at the language as did Mc-
Gillivray, but the contrast in progress was pitifully evident.

Some months after arriving in China, an old, experienced missionary came to Goforth with the following
advice: "Do not attempt to speak of Jesus the first time
when preaching to a heathen audience. The Chinese have
a prejudice against the name of Jesus. Confine your ef-
forts to demolishing the false gods and if you have a second opportunity you may bring in Jesus." Later, when
telling his wife of the advice which had been given him,
Mr. Goforth exclaimed with hot emphasis, "Never, *Never!*
NEVER! The Gospel which saved the down and outs in
the slums of Toronto, is the same Gospel which must save
Chinese sinners." From the very first, when able to speak
only in broken, imperfect sentences, he preached to the
Chinese Jesus Christ and Him crucified, and from the
first, sinners were saved from the lowest depths of de-
pravity. He based his messages always on some passage
in the Word of God. Never was he known to stand before
a Chinese audience without the open Bible in hand, constantly referring to it as "The written Word of the One
True God." In later years when asked by young missionaries as to the secret of his power in winning converts his

reply was: "Because I just give God a chance to speak to souls through His own Word. My only secret in getting at the heart of big sinners is to show them their need and tell them of a Savior abundantly able to save. Once a sinner is shown that no flesh can be justified in God's sight by the deeds of the law and that he can only attain unto the righteousness of God through faith in the Lord Jesus Christ, he readily yields. That was Luther's secret, it was John Wesley's and never did man make more of that secret than D. L. Moody." To be able to use "the sword of the Spirit" effectively, he realized the necessity of keeping it ever sharp through constant daily study of the Word.

In the spring of 1889, a native compound had been secured in Linching, an important city on the Wei River some fifty miles still nearer North Honan, our final objective. Mr. McGillivray left to oversee repairs there, and about the end of June word came that a place had been made ready for the Goforths.

The weather had begun to get exceedingly hot, and the Goforths' first summer had been in Chefoo by the sea so they really had no experience of the great summer heat of inland China. They started on this journey July 4—two days by small houseboat to Linching. The heat on the boat was so overwhelming from early morning till sundown, they were scarcely able to breathe unless sheets dipped from the river were hung around and above them.

On reaching the compound at Linching, the heat continued well over the hundred mark. There were no wire screens to protect from flies which literally swarmed everywhere. But what from the first was most trying and nauseating was a strange smell that pervaded the air. At first it was thought this came from the neighbor's courts, but the odor became worse. Then, it was discovered the coolies, carrying water for mortar, to save themselves a few steps, had been filling their pails from an indescrib-

ably filthy pool nearby, though clean water was not far
distant!

Dysentery broke out among the workmen. Mr.
McGillivray's teacher contracted it, succumbing in a few
days. Then little Gertrude, that precious first gift of God
became ill. Mr. and Mrs. Perkins (a woman doctor), had
the Goforths bring the child to their home about a half
mile away. Everything was done to save the child's life,
but about noon on July 24, she passed away. The following
letter, written by the father to friends in the homeland,
speaks for itself:

> "Gertrude Madeline is dead. Ours is an awful loss
> . . . but on July 24, she died, only six days after she
> was taken ill with dysentery. There is no burying place
> here for foreigners, so I took her body in a cart to
> Pangchwang . . . fifty miles away. . . . A Chinese ser-
> vice was conducted by the missionary. Then the rude
> coffin, covered with flowers, was borne by four Chinese
> outside the village wall. There, in the dusk of evening,
> with scores of curious heathen looking on, we laid our
> darling to rest beside two other dear little foreigners
> who were laid to sleep there before her. . . .
>
> "None but those who have lost a precious treasure
> can understand our feelings, but the loss seems to be
> greater because we are far away in a strange land. . . .
> 'All things work together for good.' The Lord has a pur-
> pose in taking our loved one away. We pray that this
> loss will fit us more fully to tell these dying millions of
> Him who has gained the victory over death."

When Goforth and McGillivray left with the little
body, the broken-hearted mother—herself stricken with
dysentery—took up her *Daily Light* and found among
the verses for that day the following: *"It is the Lord. Let
Him do what seemeth Him good"* (1 Sam. 3:18). *"The
Lord gave and the Lord hath taken away. Blessed be the
name of the Lord"* (Job 1:21).

On their return from the burial, Goforth and Mc-

Gillivray at once settled down to intense language study. Languages had always been McGillivray's best and Goforth's worst subject throughout their years of schooling. When Mr. Goforth was preaching in the chapel, the Chinese men often pointed to Mr. McGillivray, saying, "You speak, we don't understand him," pointing to Goforth.

Then, in God's own mysterious way, he performed one of His wonders in answer to prayer. One day as Jonathan was about to leave for the chapel, he said to his wife, "If the Lord does not work a miracle for me with this language, I fear I will be an utter failure as a missionary!" For a moment he looked the heartbreak that that would mean. Then picking up his Bible, he started off. Two hours later, he returned.

"Oh, Rose!" he cried. "It was just wonderful! When I began to speak, those phrases and idioms that would always elude me came readily. The men actually asked me to go on though Donald had risen to speak. I *know* the backbone of the language is broken! Praise the Lord!" About two months later, a letter came from Mr. Talling (his former roommate, still in Knox), saying that on a certain evening after supper, a number of students decided to meet in one of the classrooms for prayer, "just for Goforth." The letter stated that the presence and power of God was so clearly felt by all at that meeting, they were convinced Goforth must surely have been helped in some way. On looking in his diary, Mr. Goforth found the students' prayer meeting in Knox coincided with the experience recorded above.

Some years later, Dr. Arthur H. Smith, one of the best speakers and keenest critics of the spoken language, said to Mr. Goforth, "Wherever did you get your style of speaking? For any sakes don't change it! You can be understood over a wider area than anyone I know!"

In December, 1889, three married couples and two

single women arrived from Canada. That same evening by the authority of the Canadian General Assembly, Jonathan Goforth convened and formed the first Presbytery of North Honan, though as yet no permanent foothold had been secured in that field.

One of the snares in the path of a young missionary is the temptation to "fritter" precious time away on nonessentials, instead of bravely facing the inevitable hard task of regular language study. Many a missionary has gone through his or her missionary career with the great handicap of insufficient knowledge of either the written or spoken language because of having fallen into this trap. The following story illustrates Goforth's stand in this connection.

Among the young recruits arriving from the homeland were a Mr. and Mrs. X. Mr. X was a man with a college record equal to McGillivray's—a gold medalist, a fluent speaker, but also a clever mechanic, especially along the line of carpentry. When visiting Mrs. X., Goforth's wife often looked with envious eyes at the many clever conveniences X had made for his wife. One day she determined to coax her husband into making similar things for her. Going to him she said, "Now, Jonathan, don't you think you could leave your work for a little and do some carpentry for me like Mr. X does for his wife?"

"My dear Rose," he replied, "don't ask this of me. There are fine Chinese carpenters who could do all you want far better than I and would be thankful for the job. Besides, I have determined never to spend my time on what Chinese can do, for my work is to preach or prepare to preach the Gospel that will save souls. So, my dear, get the best carpenter going. Have him do all you require and I will foot the bill." She went away only almost persuaded, but years later, she acknowledged how that many times she had thanked God for giving her a husband always consistent in putting "first things first."

For two years, the Goforths' headquarters remained in Linching. During this time tours were made by the men into North Honan, seeking by every means to gain a foothold there.

These journeys were so full of danger that many times they experienced the Lord's hand in delivering them during those hard pioneering days. On one occasion, Goforth and an evangelist came upon a sort of fair with thousands surrounding a village theatrical. Though they were in Chinese clothing, the crowd realized they were foreigners and rushed after them. Just when things seemed hopeless, a sudden violent gust of wind blew a tent completely over. In a moment the foreigners were forgotten and the mob rushed toward the tent.

On December 19, following little Gertrude's death, a beautiful boy arrived in the Goforth home. He was named Donald, after Mr. McGillivray, and was always called "wee Donald" to designate him from Donald McGillivray.

The Goforths were moving into a foreign house which had a veranda with no railing. While things were being moved in, and everyone was busy, wee Donald began racing on the veranda and around the posts. Before he could be caught, he fell over on to the ground below, his head striking a flower pot. Though at first no apparent injury could be discovered, gradually he began to lose the use of his limbs. His parents were hoping to take the child to Shanghai as soon as the intense heat passed, but on July 25, when he was nineteen months old, he went to join the great band of other little ones in the Glory Land.

For the second time, Mr. Goforth made the journey to Pangchwang with the remains of a precious child, and there wee Donald was laid beside the grave of his sister in the little cemetery just outside the Mission compound. After his return, the Goforths prepared to move into

Honan. As soon as the great heat had broken in the latter part of August, the Goforths with their five-month-old Paul left Linching for Chuwang, their sixth home. At last they were, as a family, about to live and work together in their own field.

The town of Chuwang was in every way as undesirable a place to locate a mission as one could well imagine. The town itself was little more than a collection of broken-down mud huts. The surrounding country was poor and had been swept by floods and burnt dry by drought. It was, however, our first foothold inside North Honan. Mr. Goforth looked upon this place as a stepping-stone to the important city of Changte, about thirty miles west. For a time, vile placards could be seen everywhere depicting the hated foreigners. China seemed to be becoming more and more anti-foreign. To the south along the Yangtse River, missionaries were being driven from their stations—some failing to escape were brutally murdered. Clouds of impending danger enclosed our missionaries on all sides. In the midst of such conditions, Mr. Goforth and his colleagues went forward faithfully preaching and healing.

If the Goforths' life at Chuwang could be painted in actual colors, it would be a picture of deep shadows and bright lights. There were weeks of anxiety when Goforth lay low with typhoid fever or when he returned ill from one of his long tours. For at least one day, his life hung in the balance. On January 3, 1893, golden-haired Florence Evangeline arrived. The following summer was an intensely hot one, unusually so. One twelve-day heat spell began with 100 degrees in the shade, rising one degree higher each day till 112 degrees was reached. The break came just in time to save the life of little Paul, lying at death's door from heatstroke.

Another bright spot was Mr. Wang*:

Miracle Lives of China. By Jonathan and Rosalind Goforth.

"I rejoiced with trembling! Could it be that God had used me to lead this proud scholar into the kingdom? I have been leading him day by day since his conversion in the essential truths and am surprised at his rapid advance. I have had him witnessing in the chapel for about a month. I also have him expound tracts to the people. In this way I can detect any point on which he is not clear and afterwards instruct him. . . .

"He now wants to be set free to go about everywhere as an evangelist to preach the gospel to his fellow-countrymen. To a man of fifty this itinerating means much hardship. The Chinese inns without fires are cheerless places in winter time. One winter's night, Mr. Wang and three other Chinese and myself were put into a very small room for the night. One end was for the donkeys and pigs."

The following are a couple extracts from Goforth's letters at this time. They give vivid pictures of "touring."

"On one occasion, in company with two Evangelists, I entered a village and started to preach. From the outset they mocked me and would not listen. . . . I felt it would never do to give the devil the victory, so I opened up the Bible at Matthew 10:14, 15 and read out the riot act recorded there. *"Whosoever shall not receive you, nor hear your words, when ye depart out of that house or city, shake off the dust of your feet. Verily I say unto you, It shall be more tolerable for the land of Sodom and Gomorrah in the day of judgment than for this city."* While I proceeded to explain it a great fear seemed to come over the crowd and several said, 'Forgive us. We have been rude. If you want to speak we will listen.' I went on speaking and found them most attentive. When we were leaving they invited us warmly to return.

"It may be interesting for you to know how I go about the country. I dread laziness in the Chinese helpers. I have already seen some of it. If the foreigner rides, his

Chinese brother will also expect to ride. A Chinese may
never have been able to afford a ride before he comes to
you, but as soon as he enters upon the Mission work he
thinks it does not look well for him to walk. To meet this
innate pride and to crucify it, I determined to walk. I
bought a barrow for $4.00 and hired a man to wheel it
for about 15 cents a day. I shall not allow myself a ride
on this barrow nor shall I allow a Chinese the luxury. The
barrow conveys books and baggage, not missionaries. My
expenditure which includes barrow-man's hire, amounts
to 24 cents a day for the thirty-three days I have toured
during the past autumn. As long as I keep to the wheel-
barrow my average daily expense will never exceed 35
cents.

"I am now convinced that I can do better work by
walking. The helpers hinted that there was a more excellent way, namely, for us each to ride a donkey, but I
replied that our Master seldom enjoyed that luxury, so
they fell in with the inevitable."

The following letter comes from one of Goforth's co-
workers:

"Dr Goforth, while not an athlete, was a great walker,
and when on tour covered great distances on foot. . . .
We would start at daybreak and cover five or six miles
before breakfast. Visiting Christians as we went along,
we would walk along till noon, then on again until evening. What impressed me was that everywhere on the
road, to those who happened to be going the same way
with us, on the street of the village where we had dinner, and in the inn which we reached at night, it was
always Mr. Goforth who took the lead in telling the
Gospel message to those ready to listen. We would arrive, footsore and weary, at the end of a day's travel, at
an inn, and the crowds would gather around. While the
Chinese helpers would be drinking hot water or taking
a rest, Mr. Goforth was on his feet, bringing the Gospel
message to the crowd. After a half an hour or so, he

gave way for one of the Chinese to speak and he would rest. That is one of my earliest impressions of him, always at it and first at it."

Of the false reports hindering the work and how they were crushed, Goforth writes as follows:

"In the early part of 1893 evil stories were scattered around us like a plague. The chief of these stories was the old one of the children's hearts and eyes. The Chinese admit that the foreign physician works marvelous cures with his medicines. Their theory is that such efficacious medicine must have something very precious in its make-up. And what so precious as the hearts and eyes of children! They say that we kidnap these little ones and scoop out their eyes and cut out their hearts to manufacture our medicines. . . . Men have actually been overheard saying that they saw whole boatloads of the children unloaded at the foreigners' compounds. They said that Mr. Chou, our chief convert, was the ringleader and that he managed all the beggars for us. Each beggar was paid ten cents a day and five dollars a head for every child brought in. They advocated killing Mr. Chou and razing his house to the ground. . . . Placards were being posted up all over the country saying the worst that could be said of us, and calling upon innkeepers not to dare to give any foreigner a night's lodging. . . .

"This state of things could not be tolerated. The placards were torn down wherever found, but in some instances not without opposition. These, with other grievances, we laid before the British minister at Peking. He at once took the matter up and demanded of the high Chinese authorities that they put a stop to this reviling of missionaries lest a massacre might result. Soon proclamations were posted up throughout Changte prefecture denouncing the inventors and disseminators of these evil reports and assuring the people that the missionaries were there by treaty right and that anyone molesting them must suffer the penalty of the law. At once, as if by magic, the air cleared and a change set in, in our favor."

Here is a final, vivid picture of the hard side of village work in those days:

"This I can say that on no occasion where we stood with our backs to a wall and used the Word of God did we fail ultimately in gaining a victory. But it is anything but pleasant for a foreigner to get into the midst of a Chinese crowd without a friendly wall for backing. No one will as a rule molest him within range of his eyes. It is always the man behind his back that will shove or kick. The missionary turns around to remonstrate against such rudeness and everyone looks innocent, but just then his unprotected back comes in for more abuse. Several times I have got out of such crowds under a shower of clods and bricks. But with my back to a wall I have been able to stand as much crushing as my tormentors and have always held my ground."

6

CHANGTE AT LAST!

How often do we attempt work for God to the limit of our incompetency rather than to the limit of God's omnipotency.

Hudson Taylor

For two years, at each Presbytery, Goforth had sought for permission to secure property in Changte. But the majority felt that opening a new station would weaken the two stations already established. But Goforth kept on praying and believing for Changte. In the spring Presbytery meeting of 1894, permission was granted for the opening of Changte, but *conditionally*. The conditions were that the station must be built outside the city wall, and that Goforth must not ask either of the other stations for evangelists or help that might weaken those stations.

However, Goforth had got all he wanted—permission to go ahead. The following morning at daybreak found him on the road to Changte. His whole soul was bounding with joy. Within twenty-four hours of his reaching the city, he had received an offer for the very site he and McGillivray had often looked upon as the ideal site for a mission station! But long trying negotiations had to be gone through before the site actually became Mission property. This work, Donald McGillivray undertook, thus setting Goforth free for a brief furlough.

That summer, the whole Chuwang region was visited by great floods. The water in the Mission compound stood six to eight feet deep. The Goforths' clothes, linen, curtains and books were ruined by the dirty flood water. When the water subsided, weeks of great heat caused black mold to form on everything. Thus, for the second time, the Goforths experienced the loss of most of their possessions.

Little need be said of that first furlough. Though in Canada but a few months, Goforth addressed many meetings, sometimes eight to ten a week. But his heart was in Honan; so early in the autumn he returned, leaving his wife and three children, little Helen being but a few weeks old. On reaching Changte, he found McGillivray had successfully gone through the difficult task allotted him, and for which, with his fine knowledge of Chinese, he was so eminently fitted. The ideal site for the mission plant was actually in the hands of the Mission.

On the arrival of spring, word was sent to Mrs. Goforth to come. From the first, Goforth and McGillivray arranged between them that the former take charge of the main station, while the latter gave himself to touring.

For almost seven years, Changte had always been before the Goforths as their goal for a permanent station and home. For this they had steadfastly believed and prayed. It was therefore with great joy they started off from Chuwang early one October morning in 1895. To the three children, the long day's journey in the springless cart over bumpy uneven roads was just a picnic, but not so for their mother.

How can one describe those early days at the new station! The foreign women and children, about whom

all kinds of rumors had been circulated—mostly bad—
drew literally thousands to the Mission compound. Goforth kept extremely busy from dawn till dark. Building
operations were still in progress and as is necessary in
China, he had to measure wood, count bricks, weigh
lime, and keep a constant watch on the workmen. His
Bible, even under these circumstances, was always with
him, for opportunities that might come to sow the seed.
Besides all this, he had to preach to the crowds which
daily filled the chapel, and in the midst of this pressure,
frequently would come a note from his wife from the
women's court behind, "Do come and help me! Crowds
of women—so tired from preaching I can hardly speak!"

So back Goforth would go and together they would
sing a simple Gospel hymn written by Pastor Hsi. This
delighted and quieted the crowds for the message that
followed. And so the days went by for nearly three weeks,
when both began to realize the strain could not be kept
on indefinitely. Yet Goforth felt it was extremely important that every effort should be made to take full advantage of these first early days of curiosity which would soon
pass.

Early one morning, before the crowds began to gather,
Goforth came to his wife with his Bible open at Philip-
pians 4:19 and said, "Rose, we simply cannot stand this
much longer. I feel almost at the end of my physical
powers, and you are nearly as exhausted as I am. Now
listen, it says, 'My God shall supply all your need ac-
cording to His riches in glory by Christ Jesus.' It says,
'all your need.' Surely, we need an evangelist to help us.
Do you believe God can supply our need and fulfill this
promise to us? I do. Then let us unite in prayer that God
will send a man who can relieve me in the chapel. I can
then help you without too much strain and be able also
to look after the building." They knelt down and as he
prayed, his wife thought, "But how—how can we expect

to get a preacher? We have promised not to ask help from the other stations and we have no converts. *It is as if we were praying for rain from a clear sky!"*

But the Lord that worketh wonders heard Goforth's cry. The day following his prayer for help, Wang Fulin, a converted opium slave from near Chuwang, appeared at the Mission on his way to Changte city, seeking employment. He presented a truly pitiable spectacle. He was emaciated, his face still having the ashy hue of the "opium fiend," his form bent from weakness, a racking cough shaking his frame every few moments, and clothed or rather partly clothed, in beggar-rags. The man's story was a sad one. Since he became a Christian he could no longer carry on his "trade" of public story-telling. The family had come to a point of absolute destitution, even to the point of eating leaves off the trees. Wang Fulin had at last decided the day before (when Goforth was praying), to leave home for Changte city. Goforth did not wait to hear more, but ordering a good meal to be served the man, went back to consult with his wife. "Was this the answer to their prayers?" they asked themselves. Yet, could anyone outwardly be more unlikely? They determined, however, to try him for a few days. He could at least testify to what the grace of God could do in saving an opium slave.

Within an hour or two of his entering the Mission gate, Wang Fulin was cleansed and clothed in one of Goforth's Chinese outfits and seated in the men's chapel preaching to a large audience! From the very first day of his ministry, there was no doubt that he was the messenger sent in answer to prayer. He had in a wonderful degree the unction and power of the Holy Spirit. His natural gifts as a speaker had been developed during the many years of street story-telling. Now all was consecrated to the one object,—the winning of souls to Christ. He seemed ever conscious that his time was short and always spoke as a dying man to dying men. From the very first, men were won to Christ. Of the two first-fruits of his ministry, one was a well-known doctor and the second a wealthy landowner. For three years during those early days of stress and strain, he was spared to help in laying the foundations of the Changte Church. Then God took him. He was always remembered, later, as the "Spirit-filled preacher."

The following note of thanksgiving from Goforth was dated December 16, 1895, less than three months after the family arrived at Changte:

> "I am constrained to say 'Glory to God in the highest' for He is graciously manifesting His divine power these days. During the last five weeks we have had such a number of men coming day by day that we have kept up constant preaching on an average of eight hours a day. Wang Fulin, the converted gambler and opium smoker helps me. We take turns in preaching, never leaving the guest-room without someone to preach from morning to night. The men keep coming in in increasing numbers. I noticed once today when preaching that the guest-room was filled, while others were listening outside the door and windows. Almost every time we speak, men seem to be brought under conviction. Men will sit a whole half-day at a time listening. Some seem to get so much interested that they seem to forget that they have miles to go home after sundown. Interested ones come again and again. Each evening, when almost tired out, we have to turn men away and tell them to come the next day."

In a letter dated April 12, 1896, Goforth writes:

> "Since coming to Changte five months ago . . . 25,000 men and women have come to see us and all have had the Gospel preached to them. Preaching is kept up on an average of eight hours a day."

The Goforths had been living in a Chinese house quite unsuitable for their needs. While their new semi-foreign home was being built, the Goforths feared that it might prove a barrier between themselves and the Chinese; so they prayed that God would overrule. As with so many of their prayers, they came to see that the answer lay in their own hands. A price had to be paid—"open house to all."

The new home was completed by the fall of 1897. Its architecture was simple, Chinese on the outside while the interior was like an ordinary bungalow in the homeland. As it was the first building of its kind in that region, the house was a great curiosity to the Chinese. The board floors, the shutters and glass windows, the organ, the sewing machine, even the kitchen stove which let its smoke and gas go out through a chimney instead of through the house—all these were things of wonder. And as for the cellar! Who had ever heard of having a big hole underneath a house! And so, when it became known through the district that the foreigners were willing for people to visit their "strange house," multitudes came.

Goforth led the men through the house in bands of twenty or more at a time, and his wife took the women. But first there was the Mission compound to be explored. Dr. Menzies' pump, Paul's tricycle and the baby-carriage were the talk of the countryside.

Then Goforth would stand up on the veranda of the house and say, "Men, I have something to tell you. I want you to stand here and listen. If you go roaming about the yard and will not pay attention, I shall not let you see through the house." The house, being the main attraction, they were always ready to listen while Goforth gave a short Gospel address.

Afterward they were shown through the house. Nothing escaped their curious eyes. Beds were turned back, drawers opened, the sewing-machine examined, the organ played. The Chinese had, at that time, very large sleeves and they were very dexterous at poking knives, forks, spoons, saucers, pictures and knick-knacks up them. We took what precaution we could, but things would disappear. We found it impossible to keep a pair of foreign-made scissors about the place.

Goforth made a special point of allowing them to see the cellar and assisted them in lifting lids off every box and jar and even helped them to turn over the coal, so as to convince them we had nothing to hide from them. This did more than anything else to kill the ugly rumors about the jars of children's flesh that were supposed to be hidden in the cellar.

The high-water mark in visitors was reached one day in the fall of 1899 when 1,835 men passed through the house. On the same day, Mrs. Goforth received about 500 women. On that day the city god, Chenghwang, was to be brought out for his semi-annual visit to a temple near the Mission compound, and a great fair was to be held in connection with this important event. On the same day, thousands of government students were to assemble in the city for annual examinations.

The day, when it came, was one never to be forgotten by those at the Changte station. Goforth's wife handed him a cup of hot milk now and then, and that alone kept him going till nightfall. Sometimes there were as many as five hundred men down at the front gate clamouring to get in. Goforth would take 150 at a time.

There was one incident on this day which Mrs. Goforth always recalls with a smile. Usually she played the organ for her husband's visitors, but on this particular day she was too busy with her crowds of women, so Goforth had to be his own organist. Knowing that he could not distinguish one note from another, and hearing the organ being played, she peeped into the living room. Imagine her feelings at seeing her husband seated at the organ with all the stops drawn out, his hands pressed down on as many notes as possible, the bellows going at full blast and a crowd of delighted Chinese standing around. One remark heard above the din was, "He plays better than his wife."

Some missionaries felt that the Goforth's "open house" was a great mistake, that it meant cheapening themselves and the Mission before the people. The future, however, was to reveal abundantly the value of this policy. Deep-seated prejudices were overcome, friendly contacts were made with all classes, and many hearts were opened to the Gospel. Goforth writes, "Often the people of a village will gather around me and say, 'We were at your place and you showed us through your house, treating us like friends.' Then they will almost always bring me a chair to sit on, a table to lay my Bible on, and some tea."

In the summer of 1898 the Goforth's little daughter Gracie showed signs of a strange disease. Several months passed before the child was diagnosed to be in a hopeless condition from enlarged spleen brought on by pernicious malaria. During those last months, Gracie spent as much time in her father's arms as his work would permit. Sometimes she lay in her little carriage beside her father's desk. At such times all she seemed to crave was to gaze on her father's face or slip her little hand into his when free.

One evening, Gracie partly rose and said in a commanding tone, "I want my papa." Not wishing to disturb the tired-out father, the mother hesitated, when again Gracie said, "Call my papa. I want my papa!"

A few moments later Jonathan took his beloved little one in his arms, laying her head gently upon his shoulder as he started to pace the floor. Gracie, resting quietly in her father's arms, suddenly lifted her head and looking straight into her father's eyes gave him a wonderful, loving smile, closed her eyes, and without a struggle, was gone.

The following evening, October 3, little Gracie was buried under a tree-sheltered corner of the mission compound. On returning home, Paul was found to be ill with measles and dysentery. A week of anxiety followed, then as he began to recover, nature had her way with Jonathan who was utterly worn out. For weeks Goforth lay seriously ill with a bad attack of jaundice. He was still very ill and a sight to behold with eyes like brass or amber and a complexion not unlike that of an Indian, when the mother herself, exhausted with long nursing and overstrain, almost died during childbirth. Outside missionaries and Christians were praying for the *two* lives hanging in the balance—then joy and thanksgiving arose as the cry of a new little child was heard! Once again God had answered prayer and in the days that followed we gained our strength and health back.

One day, as a high official accompanied by a number of "underlings" was being received in the study, a loud persistent banging on the gate was heard. By the time Goforth, followed by the official and his men, had arrived on the scene, the one on the outside was making such a noise and pounding on the gate that the Chinese became alarmed. Mr. Griffith had arrived and took a stand with a club close to Goforth, ready to strike if the one outside meant mischief. The instant Goforth unlocked the gate, the man outside aimed a heavy meat chopper at Goforth's head—but Griffith was too quick and struck the weapon aside! The man was a raging maniac. The official wanted to take him to the city and execute him at once, but Goforth plead so for the poor fellow's life that he was put in charge of his family. It would probably have been better if the official had had his way, for the following day, the insane man killed his own brother. Later, he was shot. There were no asylums in China.

Something of Jonathan Goforth's "passion for preaching," his utter fearlessness, and his gift for training men, may be seen in the following extracts.

"Right here at our doors is the city of Changte with a population of about 100,000. . . . Taking Christians with me, we will go from street to street preaching and singing the Gospel in true Salvation Army style, although without the aid of flag and drum. . . . It is hard for some of these Christians to testify for Christ on the street. Some of the them have had no education and when they stand up to speak they are afraid and tremble, yet a little practice gives confidence and power. In this way we have trained about a dozen men, besides the helpers who may be called upon in an emergency. We dread 'dummy' Christians. . . .

"I have heard a man suddenly exclaim when the sun had travelled far westward, 'Oh, I've got listening to this wonderful story and forgotten all about my dinner!' . . . Night after night, when we ceased preaching to go home, I have heard one hundred to two hundred men cry out—'Stay and tell us more!' "

The strength and power of Goforth's character showed clearly in his work among the students.

"Sometimes as many as five thousand students from the five counties came up to Changte city for examinations. They were most difficult to handle. In fact, the first year, I simply did not know how to handle them, but I did the best I could.

"The students would frequently come into the chapel and gaze about them with lofty airs. On my inviting them to be seated, they would pay no heed, continuing to look around and cast knowing glances at each other. As this was causing disorder, I would say more firmly, 'Gentlemen, be seated.' My only response would be a snicker of laughter. Then, with considerable emphasis, I would again insist, 'Gentlemen, we preach the gospel in this place and cannot permit disorder. Sit down!' At this, they would bolt for the door, convulsed with laughter, upsetting all inside who were inclined to listen.

"I determined to be ready for them on their return the following year. I sent to Shanghai for a large globe and several maps and astronomical charts. The maps and charts were hung about the study, and the globe occupied a prominent place. When the students arrived, I left the preaching in the chapel in charge of Mr. Wang and invited the students back to my study. On entering, the first thing which caught their eye was the globe. Someone would exclaim, 'What is that big round thing?' I would explain it was a representation of our earth. Then several would say, 'You don't mean to tell us that the earth is round! Isn't it square and flat?' On explaining a little further and going into the movements of the earth, with a look of blank astonishment, several might exclaim, 'You surely don't mean that the earth turns over at night! Why! wouldn't we all tumble off?' Then would come the explanation of the law of gravitation—and so on, until it began to dawn upon the self-sufficient students that the foreigner had something worth listening to.

"A few enlightening geographical facts worked wonders in lowering their pride. Then, they would turn to the astronomical charts asking the meaning of the balls and circles. They all became intensely interested in every fact of astronomy given them. It was very interesting to watch the change in their attitude and the expression of their faces as we told of the sun, its size, its distance, and so on. By this time, all the pride had oozed out of the students. . . .

"The student is now teachable and will listen readily when I tell him about God the Father and His Son, Jesus Christ. Many hundreds of students were received in this way. . . ."

During the months before the crash came in 1900, the progress of the Gospel throughout the Changte region was very encouraging. By May of 1900, there were over fifty centers with a Christian community in the Changte region.

Returning from a May tour the Goforths found that

mail had suddenly stopped. They were thus cut off from any communication with the outside world. The drought continued. Night and day the air was rent by the cries of the people for rain.

In the midst of all this the Goforths' eldest daughter, Florence, a beautiful golden-haired girl, between seven and eight years of age, was taken ill. In a few days meningitis developed. Though the roads were dangerously beset by bandits, a messenger was dispatched for the nearest doctor. He left at once, but arrived only a short while before the child passed away, the evening of June 19.

7

THE ESCAPE

Who delivered us out of so great a death, and will deliver: on whom we have set our hope that he will also still deliver.

The Apostle Paul

Just after Florence died, a message came, delayed many days en route, from the American Consul in Chefoo: "Flee south. Northern route cut off by Boxers." This was followed by a still more urgent message. The missionaries yielded to the local Christians' pleas to leave and made hasty preparations for the long and hazardous journey—fourteen days by cart to Fancheng, South Honan, and ten or more days from there by houseboat to Hankow.

The day before leaving, an official courier from the north rode through Changte at breakneck speed. A burnt feather in his cap indicated his message was of life and death importance. Unknown to us then, this courier carried a sealed packet from the Empress Dowager to the Governor of Honan at Kaifengfu, ordering the massacre of all foreigners. Without knowing this, the missionaries who had planned to take the direct route south through Kaifengfu, were led, at almost the last moment to change to a much longer one running westward.

Our caravan of ten heavily laden carts left Changte before daybreak on June 27. Our large farm carts resembled gypsy wagons. Besides ourselves and our four children, the party consisted of three men, five women, one little lad and three servants.

Those first ten days seemed very hard—intense heat, springless wagons, oftentimes no place to sleep but the bare ground with a quilt beneath us. More than once the cry was heard, "Kill, kill!"

On the evening of July 7 we reached the small walled town of Hsintien. An engineer party which had joined us south of the Yellow River, decided they would not stop at Hsintien but press right on. This greatly increased our danger as the engineers had with them a mounted armed escort. They left us one mounted soldier from their escort.

The engineer party was scarcely out of sight when crowds began to gather outside the inn door which was barricaded with carts. Every moment a break was threatened by the stones hurled against it. By daybreak we could see the crowd outside was even larger.

The carters refused to move until our men drew up a statement promising full indemnity to each man for any loss of carts, animals, injuries, etc. Then they slowly and unwillingly began to harness up. While this was being done, my husband took from his pocket *Clarke's Scripture Promises* and began to read to us from where the book opened.

During the reading and through the time of prayer that followed, God's presence became wonderfully real. Every trace of agonized panic with which I had been threatened vanished, and in its place came a sweet peace.

Quietly and calmly all got on the carts. To our surprise

all was quiet—the dense crowd made no move to hinder us. My husband began to suspect something serious when no one reponded to Wallace as his father held him up before the crowd. Many times on the preceding days the Chinese love for little children had apparently saved the situation as angry looks turned to smiles and laughter as the little boy laughed and crowed at the crowds.

Just as we passed through the town gate, my husband turned pale. A crowd of several hundred men with arms full of stones and daggers at their belts awaited us. First came a fusillade of stones. Then came gunshots and the rush forward. Some of the animals had their backs broken, the carts became tangled, bringing all to a standstill.

Jumping down from our cart, my husband rushed forward shouting, "Take everything, but don't kill!" At once he became the target for the fiercest onslaught.

One blow from a two-handed sword struck him on the neck, but *the wide blunt edge* struck his neck leaving only a side bruise two-thirds around the neck. The thick pith helmet he was wearing was slashed almost to pieces. One blow severed the inner leather band *just over the temple,* a mere fraction of an inch short of being fatal. His left arm which was kept raised to protect his head, was slashed to the bone in several places. A terrible blow from behind struck the back of his head, denting in the skull deeply, that doctors said it was a miracle the skull was not cleft in two. This blow felled him to the ground. At that moment he heard a voice saying—"Fear not! They are praying for you!" Struggling to his feet, he was struck down again by a club. As he was losing consciousness he saw a horse coming down upon him at full gallop. On regaining consciousness, he found this horse had thrown his rider and fallen on smooth ground, close beside him, and kicking furiously, the animal had formed a barrier between his attackers till he was able to rise. Standing dazed, a man raised up as if to strike, but whispered,

"Get away from the carts!" By this time the thousands who had gathered to watch the attack began to crowd forward to see what they could get of our things, but the attackers felt the loot belonged to them and ceased their attack to fight for their rights. The confusion which followed gave us a chance to get away from the carts.

The cart carrying myself and the children was surrounded by fierce men, seemingly crazy to get our things. One struck at the baby's head, but I parried the blow with a pillow. Helen and the baby were with me, and Paul came running straight through the fighting crowd without getting hurt. Just then a man from behind struck at me with his dagger, but by throwing myself back I barely prevented its reaching me.

My husband, staggering and dripping with blood, came to the side of the cart saying, "Get down quickly. We must get away!" As we started off, one man relieved me of my shoes, another snatched my hat away. We were allowed to go, but only for a short distance, when a number of men began following and pelting us with stones. Putting the baby in my husband's arms I turned and pleaded for the children. Surprised perhaps that I could speak their language, they stopped and listened a moment. Then the leader called out, "We've killed her husband—let her go." With this they left us.

Not far away a village could be seen, and this we aimed at, for Mr. Goforth's strength was failing. Men and women were out in force as we neared the village. At first, the men sought to drive us away but as my husband sank to the ground apparently bleeding to death, the women all began to weep. This moved the men to pity and as I knelt beside my husband with the children weeping bitterly, they gathered around seeking to help. One man filled the great open wound at the back of the head with a fine gray powder, instantly stopping the flow of blood. Then several men joined in helping my husband into the village, to a small mud hut with one tiny window. Here they laid him on a straw mat spread on the ground. They locked us in saying it would be safer for us. Through the tiny window hot water was handed in for bathing our bruises which were becoming extremely painful, especially those at the back of my head and neck. Bowls of millet gruel and dried bread were passed in too. We could hear the men planning how at nightfall they would start off with us by cart to Hankow and so save us.

Mr. Goforth lay quite still and pale. Not for one moment during the eight hours in that hut did I cease to cry to God. About four o'clock the next afternoon Mr. McKenzie arrived and informed us that no one had been killed, but Dr. Leslie had been seriously crippled. Our little Ruth had been saved by the faithful nurse, Mrs. Cheng, spreading herself upon her and taking upon herself cruel blows meant for the child.

When Mr. McKenzie announced all were now waiting on the road for us to join them, Mr. Goforth immediately rose. As I started forward to support him, he pushed me gently from him, saying quietly, "Only *pray*. The Lord will give me strength as long as He has work for me to do." Steadily and without assistance, he walked to where our party waited.

As we were leaving the village the people crowded around as old friends. One poor old man insisted on my taking a pair of his old shoes, so worn as to scarcely hold together, saying they might keep my feet from the rough ground. Women came with old soiled children's garments, urging that the nights were cool and the children might need them.

"Why are you so kind?" one man was asked. He replied, "We are Muslims. Our God is your God and we could not face Him if we had joined in destroying you." Truly, "God moves in a mysterious way."

Joining the rest of the party we found our cart which

had held three before the attack, now had nine aboard!

As we approached Nanyangfu, crowds lined the road for a mile outside the gate. Our carts swayed, almost overturning with the pressure on them from all sides. Clods of earth and bits of brick were pelted, and that fearsome cry, "Kill, kill!" came from multitudes. Yet we passed on till the inn was reached. The open yard of this inn soon became packed with a mob of probably over a thousand.

As we left the carts, we were literally driven into one room which soon became crowded to suffocation, due to the intense heat. After an hour or more, the mob outside demanded that we be brought out. The room gradually emptied, and all the men of our party, except Dr. Leslie, with Mrs. McKenzie, her boy Douglas, our four children and myself, were lined up shoulder to shoulder on the narrow veranda.

Till darkness dispersed them, we remained facing the great seething mob. There were jeers and insults and cries of "Kill!" but no one in the crowd attacked us, though many carried weapons.

Soon after dark, the messenger who had been sent to the official with a letter demanding protection returned greatly agitated. As he was waiting for the official's answer, he overheard two soldiers discussing the official's plans for our massacre. A party of soldiers was to be at a certain place by the road and none of us were to escape. This way the official could say bandits had done the deed. So sure was this man we were all to be killed that night, he set out alone that night for North Honan and on reaching Changte, reported all of us as having been killed!

To save face and camouflage his real plan, the official sent a few soldiers *to guide us*! We started off in the dead of a very dark night. Just as we had all passed through the city gate, the carts came to a standstill, and a carter rushed up saying Paul and Mr. Griffith were not on their cart. For two hours we searched for them—but no trace of them could be found. As dawn was at hand, we decided we must go on, leaving behind one cart and a trusted servant.

While we were waiting, the soldiers had got on the carts *and had fallen asleep*. The carters too, were drowsy, and when we came to a fork in the road, the animals were left to take their own way, which was *not* the road of the ambush party. When the soldiers awoke, they were furious and returned to the city.

Our carts were surrounded and stopped probably a dozen times that morning by wild mobs. They would pull us about, searching for what might be found, but finding nothing, we were allowed to proceed. One villainous looking man with a spear led one band. At first he seemed prepared for any violence, but as he looked at our wounded men and at the little children, his heart softened with pity. Taking advantage of this, I held up the torn dirty garments and told how the Muslims had given us them. This seemed to quite overcome him. Turning to the crowd, he said, "We must not hurt these people," and then to us, "It is very dangerous for travellers; I will go with you for a way."

It was indeed a mercy he did, for the next mob was very wild. Men tried to drag our faithful nurse off our cart, but the man who had come along with us stopped them. When we were safely started again, our kind "villain" friend left us and ran ahead. Soon we came to a great friendly crowd of several hundred. Our kind-hearted friend had told them of what we had suffered, and so prepared the way for us.

Ahead of us was a large walled city. How gladly would we have avoided it, but the animals needed rest and fodder and our whole party was exhausted. One can only faintly imagine the condition of Dr. Leslie and Mr. Goforth. Their wounds, now thirty hours old, had not received any antiseptic treatment.

Our entrance into this city was a repetition of the preceding evening. It is doubtful if any thought we would ever escape from that city alive. The inn yard was large and as our carts stopped, the great crowd pressed upon us. *Again* God undertook for us! Through the crowd, two well-dressed young men of official class pressed forward shouting, "Ku-Mu-shih" (Pastor Goforth). They were sons of an official at Changte, a friend of Mr. Goforth's, who with their father had toured our home at Changte.

After a few moments of explaining our situation, the young men turned to the crowd, telling them who we were and the good we were doing. What a change came over the people! Then they ordered everything to be done for our comfort. Besides this, a message was awaiting us from the engineer party with a package of antiseptic dressings. How our hearts rose in gratitude to our Mighty Savior!

When our new-found friends learned of Mr. Griffith and Paul, they were much alarmed, but said, "You must press on without delay for the country is in an uproar. We will do our utmost to save them. If they can be found alive, we will see that they reach you." They then wrote a letter to the official at the city where we would need to stop for that night. He was a friend of their father's. They told of the condition of our party and begged him in their father's name to befriend us. And finally, these young men arranged for a semi-official man well known throughout that whole region to go with us the rest of that day. This man quieted many dangerous mobs.

At four that afternoon, a man came running to our carts with a message from the two young officials saying Mr. Griffith and Paul had been found and would reach us that night.

On reading the letter, the official at our destination promised to have an armed, mounted escort ready for us by daybreak to accompany us as far as Fancheng where we hoped to get boats. We learned later that this official's wife was a Christian.

Later, I was told that when Paul and Mr. Griffith arrived about midnight, they tried to waken me, but shaking and shouting had no effect—I had just slept on.

We started by daybreak and, with but a short rest at noon, reached Fancheng about midnight where we found the engineer's party awaiting us. After twenty-four hours in an indescribably unsanitary inn, the entire party boarded several small house-boats for the remaining ten days to Hankow.

No longer having any bedding or pillows, we slept on bare boards which became apparently harder each day. When we reached Hankow we were not allowed to go ashore, but were taken at once onto a steamer bound for Shanghai. At Shanghai our Heavenly Father marvellously provided for us again, for we were ordered to Canada on the first steamer.

The following extracts from an address by Dr. Goforth, written probably in 1901, are here given by special request:

"WHO CAUSED THE BOXER MOVEMENT IN CHINA?

We believe the first great cause of that uprising was the land-grabbing greed of the great nations. Their seizures, or proposed seizures of Chinese territory was the great irritant. . . .

Germany, filled with the idea of becoming a great colonial power . . . seized Chiaochow Bay and laid claim to the whole of Shantung, a province of one hundred and eight counties. . . .

As soon as Germany had seized Chiaochow . . . Russia . . . seized Port Arthur and claimed all Manchuria as her sphere of influence.

. . . Britain for years in public print had been telling
the world that the Yangtse valley was her sphere of
influence and that she would defend it against all com-
ers. . . .

France, too, coveted some of the Celestial Land.
She had already waged an unjust war with China and
had annexed Annam. But her greed was not yet satisfied
for she claimed the four southern provinces, Kwang-
tung, Kwanghsi, Kueichow and Yunnan as her sphere
of influence. . . .

Italy's fleet hovered around the province of Chek-
iang for months, trying to gain a foothold and hoping to
relieve China of the burden of garnering in the wealth
of such a fine province. . . .

Even little Japan . . . was not restrained from imi-
tating the land-grabbing greed of the great Christian
nations. She had already captured Formosa (Taiwan)
and proposed to absorb the province of Fukien. . . .

. . . What appeared in public print about these seizures and proposed seizures of Chinese territory was
known all over China. What were the poor Chinese to
imagine? . . .

Now apply the same treatment to ourselves. Imagine several of the big nations attempting the crying in-
justice of carving up our Dominion to gratify their greed.
It seemed to them, as a people, from the Empress Dowager down, that the only way to escape the evil was to
destroy and expel the foreigners. . . ."

8

IN GOD'S CRUCIBLE

But Thou art making me, I thank Thee, Sire.
What Thou hast done and doest Thou knowest
well.
And I will help Thee: gently in Thy fire
I will lie burning on Thy Potter's wheel—
I will lie patient, though my brain should reel.
Thy grace should be enough the grief to quell;
And growing strength perfect, through weakness
dire.

George MacDonald

Mr. Goforth was called upon far and wide in Canada to tell the story of the escape, but his main messages were along quite other lines. The church's interest in foreign missions had sadly waned. He saw, too, the great increase of worldliness in the church, and, with great sorrow and concern, he sensed the danger of the "Higher Criticism" then coming to the fore.

Many times he was heard to say, "Even before I gave myself to the Lord Jesus Christ, I had given up cards, dancing, the reading of questionable literature and other such things because I felt they were but a waste of precious time which might be spent in more worthwhile ways. After my conversion, I saw these and many other things were so many leakages of spiritual power." Many received his messages with gladness, but others, the reverse.

His heart was in China, so when arrangements had been made for some of the missionaries to reenter North Honan, Goforth left his wife and family in Canada to join in rebuilding the mission.

On July 1, 1902, Mrs. Goforth left Toronto with five children, the oldest, eleven, the youngest, Constance, eight months. Goforth and his wife had arranged that he would meet her on arrival in Shanghai. Instead, she received a telegram saying, "Goforth Typhoid Changte."

After a week of anxious waiting in Shanghai, trying in vain to get some word through by telegraph to Changte, Mrs. Goforth with her children, proceeded up the coast to Tientsin, Paul and Helen being left at Chefoo to attend the China Inland Mission schools there.

During the weeks Goforth lay ill at Changte, the post office in Peking, by some mistake, returned all letters addressed to Mrs. Goforth back to the Changte station. The result was no word other than the brief telegram at Shanghai reached her of her husband's condition, though for a whole month she waited in Tientsin daily looking, but in vain, for some word from Changte.

Then one day, Goforth appeared, having travelled the two weeks' journey from Changte alone. He was a mere ghost of himself, emaciated and still weak from his long siege of typhoid, but he was buoyantly happy.

A few days after Jonathan arrived, I could see he was just waiting for the opportunity to lay something important before me. In fact, he was simply bubbling over with eagerness.

The whole Changte region had been divided into three

distinct fields, the part allotted to Mr. Goforth being the great region northeast to northwest of the city, with its many towns and almost countless villages. With great enthusiasm my husband laid bare his plans for evangelizing this field.

"My plan," he said, "is to have one of my helpers rent a suitable place in a large center for us to live in, and that we, as a family, stay a month in the center, during which time we will carry on intensive evangelism. I will go with my men to villages or on the street in the daytime, while you receive and preach to the women in the courtyard. The evenings will be given to a joint meeting with you at the organ and with plenty of gospel hymns. Then at the end of a month, we will leave an evangelist behind to teach the new believers while we go on to another place to open it in the same way. When a number of places are opened, we will return once or twice a year."

Yes, it was a very wonderfully thought-out plan and should be carried out *if there were no children!* The vision of those women with their smallpox children at Hopei crowding about me and the baby, the constant danger to our children from all kinds of infectious diseases that this life would mean, for the common Chinese did not practice quarantining, and the thought of our four little graves—all combined to make me adamant against the plan. My one and only reason in refusing to go as my husband suggested was because it seemed a risking of the children's lives.

Oh, how my husband pleaded! Day by day in the quiet stillness of that long river journey, he assured me that the Lord would keep my children from harm. He was *sure* the Lord would keep them. He was *sure* God was calling me to take this step of faith. Then as we drew near the journey's end, he went further.

"Rose," he said, "I am so sure this plan is of God,

that I fear for the children if you disobey His call. *The safest place for the children is the path of duty*. You think you can keep your children safe in your comfortable home at Changte, but God may have to show you you cannot. But He can and will keep the children if you trust Him and step out in faith!"

We reached our Changte home on a Saturday evening. Sunday morning I left the children with faithful Mrs. Cheng, who had saved little Ruth from the Boxers' blows. Two hours later I returned and was met by Mrs. Cheng saying, "Wallace is ill." The doctor pronounced it one of the worst cases of Asiatic dysentery he had come across.

For two weeks we fought for the child's life. During that time, my husband whispered to me gently, "O Rose, give in, before it is too late!" But I only thought him hard and cruel. Then, when Wallace began to recover, my husband packed up and left on a tour *alone*.

The day after he left, my precious baby Constance was taken ill suddenly, as Wallace had been, only much worse. Constance was dying when Mr. Goforth arrived. My husband knelt next to Constance and I beside him. The little one was quietly passing when suddenly I saw in a strange and utterly new way the *love* of God—as a *Father*. All at once, as in a flash, I *knew* that my Heavenly Father could be trusted to keep my children! This all came so overwhelmingly upon me, I could only bow my head and say, "O God, it is too late for Constance, but I will trust. I will go where you want me to go. But keep my children!"

Oh, such joy and peace came that when my husband turned to me saying, "Constance is gone," I was comforted, knowing her life had not been in vain. Our little Constance's body was laid beside her two sister's graves on her first birthday, October 13, 1902.

Since Goforth's plan to open up his own field was a

most radical one, it was necessary to get the consent of his co-workers. Keen contention followed, but Goforth was sure the plan was a God-given one. He suggested as a compromise that he be allowed a three-year trial of the plan, during which time he would finance the cost himself. This was finally agreed to. As will be seen, this was all in God's plan, for it was our first step in trusting Him for the work's financial needs.

One of Jonathan Goforth's outstanding characteristics was his keen sense of justice and fairness. When the day of reckoning came for China following the Boxer outrages, word was sent from the various foreign ministers in Peking to their nationals asking for a statement of losses. Our Mission statement was to be in Canadian currency. A considerable period passed before the indemnity was actually paid and in the intervening time the currency exchange greatly altered to the advantage of the foreigner. Thus Goforth (we will not speak of others) found he received in Chinese currency much more than his claims amounted to. To keep it all would be to defraud the government. To return the extra to Peking would probably mean putting it into the pockets of whoever received it. He therefore decided to use it in some way for the benefit of the Chinese.

He purchased a piece of ground close to the mission compound and built a number of two or three-roomed Chinese cottages where employees of the mission, such as school teachers, evangelists, or hospital assistants, could live with their families. For years Mr. Goforth had felt deep sympathy for these men, who, for many months of the year were not able to see their families. A small rental sufficient only to keep up repairs was required. Each cottage had its own garden and in Chinese style both were enclosed by a high wall and main gate. "Peace Village" was completed and then handed over to the mission. Before it was completed, more than double the indemnity surplus had been expended, but Goforth had a clear conscience about it.

The touring months were from February to June and September to December. Many things needed to be adjusted to the new life, and some things loved and prized by the family had to be given up, such as flowers, bird, dog, and cat.

The general plan was to have a small native compound rented at a town, if possible, with two courts; for while Mr. Goforth was prepared to trust for the children when taking them into the new and dangerous surroundings, he determined to take every possible precaution to safeguard them.

Our manner of life and plan for work was practically the same at every center opened. Since we could not take furniture about with us, we had to be content with what was found at a place, which usually consisted of one table, two chairs, a bench for the children and the ever present "kang," a brick platform bed reaching across the full width of the room. On reaching a place, a regular routine had to be gone through. While our cook was seeing to the building of a brick stove, someone was sent for a few bundles of straw. Then curtains were quickly hung, one across the kang end of the room, the other sheltering part of the opposite end for Mr. Goforth's "study." Here an extra table, if available, was placed. Fresh newspapers came in handy for the window sills, one making a handy place for Mr. Goforth's book, the other acting as a dressing table with a mirror and toilet articles. By this time the straw had come and been laid on the kang. A few coarse straw Chinese mats over the rough bricks or uneven earthen floor and tacking up of blue cotton curtains completed our "settling."

While the above was in progress, Mr. Goforth was busily engaged with his evangelists getting the preaching place in shape. Illustrated gospel texts were pasted around the walls. A large lamp was suspended directly above the preaching platform, and, behind it or to one side, the hymn scroll was hung. This scroll had from twelve to fifteen simple Gospel hymns written in large Chinese characters on white cloth. To one side in the part roped off for women, the baby organ was placed. Then with a few chairs and as many benches as could be obtained the place was ready.

We have spoken of curtaining off a portion of the general room for Mr. Goforth's "study." This could only be done when the room was large enough. At many places he had to be content with just standing by the window with his back to the rest of the room. Though naturally there were few moments during the day when absolute quiet reigned, yet never once was his wife able to recall his having shown impatience or express annoyance at the noise. Mr. Goforth's habits of study and prayer were as regular under these conditions as when at home in Changte. He always rose at five in summer and six in winter. Ten minutes were given to the "daily dozen," and within half an hour of rising, he had started his intensive Bible study with pencil and notebook. Breakfast was always at seven o'clock sharp. From eight to nine a Bible study class was held with his evangelists. Then with his band of Chinese helpers, street preaching began. When distant places were visited they would be away all day.

In starting work at a new center, he made it a rule always to take a fresh passage of Scripture each time he addressed a heathen audience.

We have spoken of Goforth's *day* schedule, but the evening meeting was always the great meeting. This was held for the most part in a large unused shop which opened entirely to the street. One evangelist was appointed to explain a hymn, taking each evening a new hymn and explaining it verse by verse, the verse being sung perhaps half a dozen times before going on to the next; then when

the last verse was ended, going back to sing the hymn
right through. Short gospel addresses, and more hymns,
kept the crowds steady. The evangelists were often kept
till after midnight dealing with enquirers.

As Mr. Goforth frequently stated, "Every new place
without one exception where we lived as a family for at
most one month and carried on this aggressive evangelism, we left behind what later became a growing church."

This country life, while hard on the flesh, was one of
constant opportunities to see *what God could do*. To il-
lustrate this, one story out of many, is as follows:

It was our third or fourth visit to Pengcheng, an important center twenty miles northwest of Changte. A large
straw-mat tent had been erected as Christians from the
surrounding region were to gather for the special meetings. Heavy rain had soaked the tent causing it to leak
like a sieve. As we arrived, the weather turned bitterly
cold and windy. The tent was like an icehouse in spite of
two stoves going.

Almost at once Mr. Goforth caught a severe cold which
rapidly grew worse, with high fever, severe pains in his
head and chest, and difficulty in breathing. In spite of
my protests he insisted on taking his meetings, but about
the third day he came in at noon looking so very ill I
became alarmed. He would eat nothing, and lay down,
saying he would be ready for the afternoon meeting.

I was in despair. Then thinking Mr. Goforth was
asleep, I slipped out and sent a messenger around to call
the Christians to the tent. When they had gathered, I
told them of my anxiety and of Mr. Goforth's symptoms.
As I ended by saying, "Oh, pray for him!" I broke down
and wept. Oh, what prayers then arose—earnest, heart-
felt prayers such as I had never heard! I thought, "Surely
God will hear such prayers!"

This continued for some time, then fearing Mr. Goforth might arrive, I gave out a hymn. A few moments

later he walked into the tent in his old brisk way, looking quite well. As soon as I could get to him at the close of the meeting I said, "Jonathan, you seem quite better." He replied, "Praise God, I am." He then told how a short time after he had heard me go out the fever seemed to leave him, his head and chest ceased to hurt, he could breathe easily and he felt quite well.

Our first trip to Wuan was exceedingly difficult. We were supposed to travel by cart twenty miles, but when the carts began to overturn on the bumpy road, we were forced to walk. Some parts of the road were so bad Mr. Goforth had to help the carters lift the carts over large rocks. When we finally arrived, we could eat nothing at all that night; we were so utterly exhausted. The next morning, when attempting to rise, one of the ladies fainted—the other felt the effects of that journey for many months.

Quite early that first morning, the City Official, Mr. Yen, arrived with his assistants. He sternly rebuked Mr. Goforth for having brought women and children over such roads in *carts*. He ended by saying, "From now on my official sedan chairs are at your disposal. If you do not make full use of them, both coming and going, I will consider it a personal offense."

Mr. Yen and his wife later became warm and intimate friends. Mr. Yen once said to Mr. Goforth, "I cannot understand how this Bible you gave me can have such power. Before I began to read it, I frequently gave unjust judgment in court for gain. Now I must judge justly or I cannot sleep!"

9

REVIVAL

*Verily, verily I say unto you, He that believeth on
me, the works that I do shall he do also; and greater
works than these shall he do.*

Our Lord Jesus Christ

Jonathan Goforth was nearing his forty-fifth milestone
when a strange restlessness seemed to take possession of
him. He dwelt much with his wife on the verse at the
head of this chapter, and he earnestly longed to see in
his ministry the "greater works" promised. Mr. Goforth
had, up to this time, been undoubtedly a "successful"
missionary, but he himself was never satisfied with what
he felt to be just touching the fringe of the appalling
multitudes needing Christ.

Some unknown friend in England began sending us
pamphlets on the Welsh revival. Scenes of that marvelous
movement were vividly described. Eagerly Mr. Goforth
looked for these pamphlets, which, for a considerable
time, came weekly. While reading them aloud to his wife,
he was repeatedly so thrilled and moved with emotion
that he could scarcely proceed. A new conception was

coming to him of God the Holy Spirit and His part in the conviction and conversion of men.

At this time, far off in India, Dr. Margaret McKellar, whom we had not seen nor corresponded with since our student days, was led of God to send Mr. Goforth a little booklet entitled *A Great Awakening*. Never can I forget the day this blessed leaflet reached us. We were living in a large "barn" of a room at Tsichou, 14 miles north of Changte. The children were playing on the great platform bed at one end of the room when Jonathan came to me with the leaflet, saying, "This is a remarkable booklet. It contains selections from Finney's 'Lectures on Revival.' Just listen to this." He read from the front page of the second part as follows (we give the passage in full because this was the factor God used to change his entire life and ministry):

"A revival is a purely philosophical result of the right use of constituted means. It is not a miracle, nor dependent upon a miracle. There has long been an idea prevalent that promoting religion has something very peculiar in it, not to be judged by the ordinary rules of cause and effect. No doctrine is more dangerous than this to the prosperity of the Church. Suppose a man were to go and preach this doctrine among farmers, about their sowing grain. Let him tell them that God is a sovereign and will give them a crop only when it pleases Him, and that for them to plow, and plant, and labor as if they expected to raise a crop, is very wrong, and taking the work out of the hands of God. And suppose the farmers should believe such doctrine. Why, they would starve the world to death. Just such results would follow the Churches' being persuaded that promoting religion is somehow so mysterious a subject of Divine sovereignty, that there is no natural connection between the means and the end. I fully believe, that could facts be known, it would be found that when the appointed means have been rightly used, spiritual blessings have been obtained with greater uniformity than temporal ones."

Again and again he read the passage. The children became hushed and gathered about us, sensing something unusual. At last, my husband said, "It simply means this: The spiritual laws governing a spiritual harvest are as real and tangible as the laws governing the natural harvest." Then, solemnly, almost as if making a vow,— "If Finney is right, and I believe he is, I am going to find out what these spiritual laws are and obey them, no matter what the cost may be."

At once, he sent home to Canada for A. J. Gordon's *Ministry of the Spirit*, S. D. Gordon's *Quiet Talks on Power*, *The Autobiography of Charles G. Finney*, and *Finney's Lectures on Revival*. In the meantime, he bought a two-inch margin Chinese Bible and set himself to an intensive study of the Holy Spirit, making full notes on the wide margin of his new Bible. Soon he began to use these notes as outlines for sermons.

A short time after the booklet had reached us, we returned to Changte, and Mr. Goforth became more and more absorbed in his intensive study of the Holy Spirit. Every possible moment, he gave himself to his work, rising before six, sometimes five, to get unbroken time at his Bible. I became anxious and one day when entering his study I found him on his knees with Bible and pencil before him. "Jonathan," I said, "are you not going too far in this? I fear you will break down!" Rising, and putting his hands on my shoulders, he faced me with a look I can never forget. I can only describe it as "glorious" and yet sad, as he said, "Oh, Rose, even you do not understand! I feel like one who has tapped a mine of wealth! It is so wonderful! Oh, if I could only get others to see it!" From that time on, I could only step aside, as it were, and watch.

The latter part of the following February, Mr. Goforth left for the great religious fair at Hsunhsien. It was estimated that more than a million pilgrims climbed the hill outside that city during the ten days of the fair for worship of the great image, Lao Nainai (Old Grandmother). This fair was by far the greatest opportunity of the year for reaching numbers with the Gospel and all missionaries and native evangelists possible gathered there for intensive evangelism.

One evening he spoke to a heathen audience in the street chapel on "He bore our sins in His own body on the tree." Conviction seemed written on every face. When asking for decisions, practically everyone stood up. Then turning about, seeking for one of the evangelists to take his place, he found the whole band of ten standing in a row with awed looks. One whispered, "Brother, He for whom we have prayed so long, was here in very deed tonight."

Soon after his return to Changte, Mr. Goforth clashed severely with one of his colleagues. Both men had strong wills and each felt he was right. Finally, they were persuaded by other missionaries to meet alone, and on their knees, the matter seemed peaceably settled. But there remained in Goforth's heart a secret sense of resentment amounting, in reality, to unforgiveness. On the eve of starting on a long communion tour of his stations, he became convicted of his hypocrisy, and after a time of quiet confession and humbling of himself before the Lord, all un-Christian feeling toward his brother vanished, and love reigned. Then, as he went forward on that long tour, God used him mightily.

For more than a year, until the spring of 1907, Mr. Goforth continued his work with outstanding success, but with no vision or thought beyond his own field. When Presbytery met, Mr. Goforth was chosen to accompany our foreign mission secretary, Dr. R. P. MacKay on his trip to Korea.

After three weeks' visiting the main centers in Korea, they returned to China, taking the northern overland route through Manchuria. Three mission stations were visited en route. At each place Mr. Goforth spoke in impromptu meetings arranged for them. He simply told of what they had been seeing in Korea of the Holy Spirit's working. At each place he received earnest requests that he return to hold a ten days' mission. When for the third time the same invitation came, Mr. Goforth began to wonder whether "the thing was of God," and promised if the way opened, he would return.

When Goforth laid the whole matter before the Honan Presbytery, and asked for permission to accept the call to Manchuria, some were strenuously opposed to his going. After long discussion, it was finally decided to allow him freedom from his field for *one month, including travel*. Six months, however, passed before he was finally free to leave. Not until seated on the train did he fully realize the magnitude of the task before him. He reckoned that at least forty different addresses must be given. Feeling overwhelmed, he began to pray for the Lord's help in getting outlines into shape. Then the inner Voice spoke in an unmistakably clear way, "Give them just what I have given you." He obeyed, and all his addresses in Manchuria were from the closely written notes on the margin of his Chinese Bible, jotted down during the time of his intensive study of the Holy Spirit.

The following picture of Jonathan Goforth at the time of his revival ministry in Manchuria comes from Rev. James Webster who accompanied Mr. Goforth from place to place during the revival.

"We heard, to begin with, of the revival movement through which the Korean Church has passed, the rapid progress of Christianity in the Hermit Kingdom, the amazing increase of converts, the strength and independence of the churches, the number of schools and colleges, all established within the past few years, and all self-supporting.

"He was as well versed in the statistics of our church as in that of Korea. There followed a merciless comparison between the progress there and here during the last decade—a very humiliating contrast. He had not come to praise up the Manchurian mission, but asked us to inquire seriously the cause for the extraordinary difference. . . .

"The watchword of . . . Mr. Goforth's message . . . was *'Not by might, nor by power, but by my Spirit.'* This doctrine, presented in many aspects, iterated and reiterated, amply illustrated, emphasized and pressed home, has been his one theme in Manchuria. He has not dealt in abstract theories about the work of the Holy Spirit. 'We speak that we do know and testify that we have seen.' There is a note of certainty about it all. He is perfectly sure of it in his own mind, and he says it out with all his might. He believes that idolatry and superstition are not the fruits of the Spirit and he says so. He believes equally that men and women who have been baptized in the faith of Christ, but are still living under the influence of hatred, jealousy, uncleanness, falsehood and dishonesty, pride, hypocrisy, worldliness and avarice, are living in that which is in active opposition to the Spirit of God. While living under the influence of these, and cherishing them in the heart, men and women bearing the name of Christ can obtain no such blessing as has come to the Korean Church. . . .

"The Cross burns like a living fire in the heart of every address. What oppresses the thought of the penitent is not any thought of future punishment, but their minds are full of the thoughts of their unfaithfulness, of ingratitude to the Lord who has redeemed them, of the heinous sin of trampling on His love. . . ."

Jonathan Goforth went up to Manchuria an unknown missionary, except to his own narrow circle. He returned a few weeks later with the limelight of the Christian world upon him. But for the grace of God, the suddenness of it would have been his undoing. But Goforth, God's servant, quietly, calmly, and humbly met the calls for revival missions which began to pour in from all parts of China. The Honan Presbytery, in the spring of 1908, decided that Goforth should be freed for revival work—at least for a time.

Preparations at once began for the break-up of our home, for it had been decided by Presbytery that I should return to Canada with the children. A few days before the break came we were walking in front of our home at Changte, feeling keenly the prospect of a long separation. I determined to see how far my husband would go in putting God's work first in his life, so I said, "Jonathan, I'm going to ask you a straight question. Suppose I were stricken with an incurable disease in the homeland and had but a few months to live. If we cabled you to come, would you come?"

He hesitated before answering. "You are asking me to face an issue which we hope may never come."

"But," I persisted, "*would you come?*" He saw I was in earnest and must be answered.

After hesitating some moments—perhaps praying— he said, "Suppose our country were at war with another nation and I, a British officer in command of an important unit. Much depended upon me as commander as to whether it was to be victory or defeat. Would I, in that event, be permitted to forsake my post in response to a call from my family in the homeland, even if it were what you suggest?"

"No, Jonathan," I replied, rather sadly. "I must confess you could not, for a soldier's first duty is to king and country."

Much that followed was too sacred for these pages, but finally Mr. Goforth ended by turning to his Bible. He read: "As his share is that goeth down to the battle, so shall his share be that tarrieth by the stuff: they shall share alike" (1 Sam. 30:24). "And remember," he went on, "*your promise was always to let me put the Lord and His work first.*"

A week later, the mother with five children, the youngest, Frederic, two years of age, started on the long homeward journey while Goforth gave himself wholly to the revival missions. He sometimes spoke to 1000 at a time, and Dr. Hunter Corbett, the oldest missionary in China, said he had never heard such praying.

Stories of Mr. Goforth's revival missions have already been recorded by himself in *By My Spirit*. The writer, therefore, has decided to give in these memoirs simply two pictures of the revival movement as it reached and affected Goforth's own station of Changte.

The first of these pictures is from Dr. Murdock McKenzie.

"There is but one word can express our experiences during these days, and that is 'Wonderful!' What has happened? Nothing more than God has promised from the beginning—when the Holy Spirit is poured out He will convict the world of sin. . . .

"On Monday morning, his text was from Rev. 3:15, 'I know thy works that thou art neither cold nor hot.' After the addresses an opportunity was given for prayer, when several broke down in tears unable to proceed. One made public confession of his sins and asked God's forgiveness. In the afternoon the text was from John 11:30, 'Take ye away the stone,' and a powerful appeal was made to all to allow nothing to hinder them from receiving the blessing.

"An opportunity was then given for prayer, and thereupon ensued such a scene as never before had I seen, nor again do I expect to see. A man started to pray, but had not said more than half a dozen words when another, then another joined in, and in a moment the whole company was crying aloud to God for mercy. . . .

"Nothing in my mind can more fitly describe the scene than to compare it to the suddenness and violence of a thunderstorm. . . .

"Some were praying for help to confess their sins, and to allow nothing to be unconfessed. Some could only sob, 'O God, forgive me; O God, forgive me!' Some were imploring the Holy Spirit not to leave them. As the days passed there was added confidence in tone, due to the increasing knowledge of the power of prayer. . . .

"When prayer was asked for the Emperor and Dowager Empress, who were ill, an immediate and hearty response was made. There was no confusion, no seeming incongruity in all praying aloud at the same time, it seemed a most natural way to approach God. Never did we realize the power of prayer as we did at that time. The whole atmosphere was one of prayer. . . .

"That which weighed most heavily on the consciences of all was that we had so long been grieving the Holy Spirit by not giving Him His rightful place in our hearts and in our work. While believing in Him we had not trusted in Him, to work in and through us. Now we believe, we have learned our lesson that it is 'not by might, nor by power, but by my Spirit saith the Lord of hosts.' May we never forget that lesson."

We prize equally with Dr. McKenzie's story the following account of the Changte Revival by Dr. Percy C. Leslie.

"Eighth day, Sunday: Great throngs today; well on to seven hundred in the morning. Men crowded to the front to make confession and no time was obtained until afternoon for Mr. Goforth to make an address. It is becoming more difficult to bring the meetings to a close. Indeed, it is one long meeting, lasting all day, with intermissions for food. Each meeting lasts about three hours and an eager crowd awaits the call for the next. . . .

"Tenth and last day, Tuesday: Confessions and prayers filled up most of the time. . . .

"One of the indications of the sincerity and intensity of the prayers, was the brevity of most of the petitions;

having prayed for the request suggested, they stopped.

". . .It was pitiful to see the distress of some of these men, strong characters, pillars of the church, weeping in the presence of men because they had been in the presence of God and His light had revealed them to themselves; the rank and file also, men with paltry sins to acknowledge, others with blood on their hands, all with tender consciences, conscious of sin against God and only hoping for His forgiveness. Confessions that torture could not wring from men, sins and faults that a few days ago they would not accept reproof for, now they willingly and openly confess. The missionaries were not exempt, and not a few took their places with the other 'penitents' in acknowledging shortcomings. Surely 'the Lord shall sit as a refiner and purifier.' "

10

FURLOUGH AND BACK AGAIN

He has no enemies, you say?
My friend, your boast is poor:
He who hath mingled in the fray
Of duty, that the brave endure,
Much have made foes. If he has none
Small is the work that he has done.

Anon.

Early in 1909, Goforth left for Canada via London, where he was scheduled to give a series of addresses on "Prayer" for the China Inland Mission. While in London, he was taken to see an invalid lady. She told Mr. Goforth that when she heard of his proposed meetings in Manchuria, she had felt a great burden laid upon her to pray for him. She then asked him to look at her notebook, in which was recorded three dates when a sense of special power in prayer had come upon her for him. A feeling akin to awe came upon Goforth as he recalled those dates as being the very days when he had witnessed the mightiest movements in Manchuria.

At the close of his week's meetings in London, Mr.

Goforth left for Canada, reaching his home in Toronto but a few days before the General Assembly. He came back to Canada full of hope that he might see in the beloved homeland similar evidences of the Holy Spirit's working as he had been witnessing in China. Much time was given to prayer during the days preceding the General Assembly. When at last he rose before that great audience of ministers and church leaders, Goforth spoke for twenty minutes with power and intensity, and a marked stillness reigned throughout his address. His plea was for them to humble themselves and seek the Holy Spirit's outpouring as did the Korean missionaries.

The message was welcomed by some with hope and gladness; by others, it was received with distinct opposition. The former saw in Goforth a Spirit-filled man of vision who feared not the face of man. To the latter, however, he was a fanatic to be shunned. During the next ten months very few churches opened their doors to Jonathan Goforth for revival missions. To those who did, tokens of blessing came, but only in small measure. Had Goforth lost the Divine empowering? Or were God's children unwilling to pay the price of full surrender? Who can say? On the whole, the 1909–1910 furlough was to Goforth a great disappointment.

The World's Missionary Conference was to meet in Edinburgh, June, 1910, and as Mr. Goforth was appointed a delegate, it was decided the Goforths as a family should return to China by way of England.

While Mr. Goforth was known by name in Britain through reports of the revivals in China and Manchuria, so many distorted stories had been circulated concerning him, it is doubtful if any openings would have come for him to speak in Britain, had it not been for Mr. Walter Sloan of the China Inland Mission. By practically guaranteeing Mr. Goforth, he succeeded in getting a number of important doors open to him. The most important was the ten days at Spurgeon's Tabernacle in London and the week at Keswick. At this latter convention, Goforth shared with Dr. S. D. Gordon the main morning hour, each having a large tent holding a thousand or more. For the first two or three days of the Keswick meetings, it was clearly discernable that Mr. Goforth was "on trial." Then confidence and interest steadily grew.

The Keswick Executive met on the last Saturday evening and requested that Mr. Goforth remain a year in Britain, holding meetings as a Keswick missioner, his salary and all expenses to be met by them. The deputation stated that all the committee had realized that *his message was the message of Keswick*. Goforth would have accepted this offer at once, but the consent of the Board in Toronto must be obtained. A cable was sent, but the answer was in substance, "Return to China. Your field is there." Without an objection Goforth obeyed.

When Goforth returned to China in August of that year, he was anxious to return to his revival ministry fulltime. The Home Board, however, in conjunction with the North Honan Presbytery, had decided that he must give more time to the work in Honan and less to revival. Therefore, for more than a year, the Goforths' headquarters was at Weihuifu, the central station of the Mission. Many country tours were made by them, but without the children. During this period, about half of Mr. Goforth's time was given to the outside Revival missions, for the Lord continued to use him as a revivalist.

Glad, indeed, were the Goforths when the June, 1914, Presbytery decided they should return to Changte and take over their old field. Goforth found himself faced with a serious handicap. During his absence from the field, Presbytery had made a rule allowing only two missionpaid evangelists to one missionary. When Mr. Goforth had left his field almost five years before, he had led a band of fifteen trained evangelists, but fourteen of these

were now working with other missionaries. He could have
asked for the return of some of these, but with his characteristic generosity he decided to start again, believing
that in some way the Lord would raise others up.

A sadness comes over me as I attempt to write of this
period in Jonathan Goforth's life. I knew, as none other,
the sorrow and heartache he felt as he learned of the
inroads of higher criticism, "the modern menace," was
making in the homeland, and also because of the increasing evidence of its reaction on the foreign field. He felt
powerless to stem the tide and resolved to preach, as
never before, salvation through the Cross of Calvary and
demonstrate its power in his own life.

During the five years of Goforth's absence from his
field, many of the centers which were but small groups
of Christians when he left were now growing churches.
He could well have spent all his time visiting these
churches, but the pioneer spirit within him urged that
he open new centers each year. How gladly would I tell
the full story of those two wonderful years! Some of these
stories are told by Mr. Goforth himself in *Miracle Lives
of China*. We have space here to tell just a little.

The latter part of August, following our return to
Changte, we started for the small village of Suntao, eleven
miles north of Changte. The only helpers Mr. Goforth
had with him were old Mr. Tung, a good, saintly man,
but weak physically; the other, Hopinfu, young and in-
experienced.

The room we lived in in Suntao was of the "barn"
class. On one occasion it contained a coffin. I would not
enter until Mr. Goforth lifted the lid and assured me it
was empty! It made an excellent receptacle for papers
and a desk large enough for both when closed.

But to return to the first visit. We rented an empty
shop just opposite for a preaching hall, and crowds began
to come from the outset. After three days' constant

preaching, Mr. Goforth became so hoarse he could scarcely speak. His need of immediate relief was imperative.

A messenger was sent to Changte, asking for help. In response, several evangelists arrived, on loan. Goforth tells how, "the burden for evangelists became so heavy, it was like a weight forcing me to my knees. I told the Lord that He was the Lord of the harvest and that He must send more harvesters. There was a time of intense looking to God, almost amounting to agony, and then the burden lifted and I knew that God had answered." He came to me with all strain and anxiety gone, saying, "I am as sure the Lord is going to give me evangelists as if I saw them before me now."

When our landlord's eldest son, who had been away for some time, returned, he was furious to learn the back courts had been rented to "Foreign Devils." He owned and managed a gambling den adjoining his father's store, but as the gamblers all spent their evenings at the preaching hall, the place had to be closed. The fellow vowed he would not listen to the preaching, but some of the preachers, as well as Goforth, had loud, carrying voices and their every word could be heard in the shop. One hymn ended each verse, "He died for me." It was a great favorite and was sung almost every night. Try as he would, the young man could not get away from the words, "He died for me." Ashamed that others should see him listening, he would hide in the dark outside the preaching hall and listen. One night, he was walking home across the fields alone. Looking up to the starlit heavens, he cried, "God in heaven, I believe what they say of you is true— that there is no other God." Going on a distance, he stopped and cried, "If Jesus is your Son, and if He can save me, give me a vision that I may know for sure." That night he dreamed a wonderful Being stood beside him and said, "Jesus is the Son of God and Jesus alone can save you."

The next day, when the preaching began, to the surprise of everyone, young Chen seated himself on one of the front benches. Day by day he came, morning, afternoon and evening. Before many days had passed he came out boldly for Christ. He became one of Mr. Goforth's most earnest evangelists and continued so till his death a few years later.

Among the men born into a new life on that first visit to Suntao were robbers, gamblers, opium addicts, and others bound by chains by vicious habits. We have given considerable space to the above story because it is characteristic of many other centers. Of that first visit to Suntao, Mr. Goforth wrote later:

"A year ago I prayed the Lord for evangelists and received an assurance He would answer my prayer. Now, what is the result? The Lord has sent me two Chinese B.A.'s, both excellent speakers. He moved a consecrated elder to give up his business at great loss to himself, for the preaching of the gospel, and this man has been appointed by the mission as my evangelist. A scholar, who was an opium user and a gambler, was converted at Sun Tao last year. His progress has been most remarkable and it looks as if he is going to make one of the front rank preachers. Also, two brothers, who were among the first converts last year, helped me in the preaching, and their father, also a convert of last year, provides their food."

Great was our joy to find, when visiting places opened years before, great changes had come in the attitude of the people, high and low, toward us. A notable instance of this was at Pengcheng. It was not an uncommon thing during the early visits to that city to be spat upon when on the street. But on our last visit, we were received outside the town by a deputation of the city's leading men, who escorted us to a temple which had been prepared for us by pushing the idols back into the shadows, while the front, sunny part had been swept and garnished for our occupation. Government school students, of low and high schools, were brought by their teachers to hear the Gospel!

Young Hopinfu came to be of great help to us. He designed and directed the making of a traveling gospel tent which cost much less and was more suitable to our needs than a foreign tent. He was proving himself more and more invaluable to us in many ways.

Nevertheless, modernism destroyed Hopinfu, a promising young evangelist. We sent Hopinfu to a summer training school in Weihuifu. After returning in autumn, he came to Mr. Goforth and said, "Pastor, the first Epistle of Peter was the study, Mr. ——— [a modernist] took with us this summer. I have listened to you for three mornings and if you are right, he is wrong. . . . The foundations have gone from under me. I am leaving. I join the army."

It will be remembered that one of the conditions of Goforth being allowed by the Presbytery to work his new plan in opening up his field north of Changte was that he must finance any extra expense himself. As time passed and new centers were opened, each place meant added expense in rent and upkeep. Mr. Goforth had never, up till this time, received any money from any source for the work except through the regular mission channels. About the time the third center was opened, the need for financial help began to be keenly felt.

Just at this juncture, a letter reached us from a Miss C. Dinwoodie in Australia, a perfect stranger—indeed, we could never discover how she had heard of us. This lady sent a check for fifty pounds, saying she wished to become partners with us in the Lord's work. She stated very plainly that her donation was not for the general running of the Mission, but was to be used by Mr. Goforth in his own work and she asked that in his accounts the word "Investor" be used in place of her name. This dear, God-raised-up partner, for years stood behind us while we were in need of financial aid, though we never wrote to her telling of any special need, her gifts always came at crucial times.

Once when we had been in the country some weeks, Mr. Goforth remarked that if money did not come we must draw on our salary, our special fund being exhausted. To this, his "little faith" of a wife strenuously objected. Finally, the husband had the last word, "Oh, let us trust Him. Who knows but that a check is awaiting us at Changte?" On reaching home a pile of mail was heaped up on the dining table. Opening the first letter, I read: "Dear Mrs. Goforth, I am a stranger to you. I've never seen you or your husband. I am a Methodist, not a Presbyterian, but I have an old mother, not very well, who has got the idea into her head that you need money. So to quiet her I am sending you the enclosed check for fifty dollars. I hope you will find some use for it."

Oh, how humbled I felt! For several moments I could not summon up the courage to hand the letter to my husband, for I expected to hear him say, "I told you so." The good man, on reading it, just smiled. Some months later a second letter came from this same lady in answer to my acknowledgment: "My mother was dying when your letter came, but she was able to take in all you wrote. The joy of knowing she had been God's channel to help you in China carried her joyfully through those last three days before she passed away." Mr. Goforth's faith never seemed to waver, even when, as a family, times of severe testing came. He would never borrow, nor ever go in debt, and God always honored His servant's trust in Him.

Before going on to a distinctly new period in Goforth's life, we must first give the story of how God gave him one who became his fellow-laborer in the Gospel for more than twenty years—till the end of Dr. Goforth's career as a foreign missionary.

Soon after our return to Changte, a young missionary who had been put in charge of the Changte City preaching hall for non-Christians, came to Mr. Goforth for advice, saying the attendance at the chapel had dwindled till scarcely anyone came. Mr. Goforth then suggested the following plan: that the city official, a friend of his, be asked to give them the best possible site for the erection of a tent and that a month's aggressive evangelistic campaign be carried on, partly for Christians and partly for non-Christians. Mr. Goforth promised to give a month for the leading of this mission.

The plan was carried out, the official giving a great open court, in front of the Chenghwang Miao—Temple of the city god—which was tented in, holding a thousand people. My twenty-four stop organ was carried to the tent, also the church benches, banners, hymns, scrolls, and pictures.

Su Chuanting, or Mr. Su, as we call him, was passing the tent in a 'rickshaw. When he heard strange sounds coming from the tent, he said to the 'rickshaw man, "What's that?" The reply came, "It's the foreign devils, holding some kind of a circus." Mr. Su had been drinking and was quite intoxicated. Paying his fare, he walked unsteadily into the tent and looked in wonder and amazement at the foreign woman playing at a box and a foreign child with his violin. He started up to the front and seated himself on the very front seat to get a good view of this strange circus!

Mr. Goforth rose and read from his Chinese Bible: "This is a faithful saying and worthy of all acceptation, that Jesus Christ came into the world to save sinners" (1 Tim. 1:15). Mr. Goforth began by telling what "sinner" meant. Mr. Su later told how angry he became that this foreign devil would dare tell all the people about him, and, literally, show up all his sins and faults. Then, gradually, as he became sober, the truth went home and when the invitation was given for any who believed what had been said, to indicate it by raising the hand, he looked around, expecting, as he afterward said, that every hand would be up, for it seemed so wonderful to him. But there were none, and saying to himself, "The cowards," he himself put up his hand.

The following day he came to Mr. Goforth, saying, "Pastor, take me with you everywhere you go. I want to learn the secret of how it could be possible when last night as I stood in the inquiry room, my whole past life seemed to drop from me as a garment. I have no desire for those things which bound me with chains. I want to learn this secret that I may help others."

Mr. Su gave up a good salary and started off with Mr. Goforth, for a long time barely getting his food. Mr. Su never went back, and made such astounding progress in the following twelve months, the other evangelists came to Mr. Goforth, asking that Mr. Su might lead a Bible class with them. We shall hear more of Mr. Su in Manchuria.

11

GOSPEL NOMADS

Measure thy life by loss and not by gain,
Not by the wine drunk but by the wine poured
*   forth;*
For love's strength standeth in love's sacrifice—
And he who suffers most has most to give.

The Sermon in the Hospital

Throughout 1915 it was evident to all, as he was persistently attacked by abscesses and carbuncles, that Mr. Goforth must slacken his pace. In spite of the pleadings of his wife, the advice of his colleagues, and the warning of Dr. Leslie, he just smiled and kept going.

During that autumn, Mr. Goforth's alma mater, Knox College, conferred upon him the honorary degree of Doctor of Divinity.

Mr. Goforth had promised to hold revival meetings south of the Yangtse River. The journey promised to be a hard one, and the trip was to take several months. But difficulties and danger never weighed for a moment on Mr. Goforth. They did, however, weigh now on his wife, who at this time felt very much below par. Yet how could she allow her husband to go off in the condition he was, *alone*. One hour it was "go," the next, "stay." The very afternoon before Mr. Goforth was to leave, the last decision had been to *stay*.

Little Mary took matters into *her* hands. Cutting out several pieces of paper the same size, she wrote "stay" on some and "go" on others. She brought them to me in a hat saying, "Mother, you just must go with father! Now draw." I drew and the paper said, "go." Delighted with the result, the child put the slips in a book and again commanded me to draw! I playfully drew and the result was again "go." As she prepared for another try, I inwardly determined that this last would settle the question, though I had persistently said I was *not* going. Again she brought the papers arranged for me to draw and again the slip said "go." The children were put in Mrs. Griffith's care till they left for school in Chefoo, and the following morning we started out on that long, strenuous, and fateful journey.

At the close of ten days of meetings in Yuan Chow, we started in chairs over the mountains. That whole region was indescribably beautiful. Every turn in the road brought fresh vistas of mountain ranges and valleys lit up with rich colors. A frequent combination of trees was the almost black, heavy, camphor tree, with the tall, pale-green, feathery bamboo, and other trees of deep green, all closely grouped together. The gold-green rice fields in the valleys stood out in beautiful contrast to the patches of red soil up the mountain sides.

After six days, we arrived at Iyang. Ten full days followed. Three meetings a day besides many interviews kept Mr. Goforth strained to the utmost. The old alarming symptoms began to appear. We visited two more places, with long journeys between, then a carbuncle forced Dr. Goforth to enter a hospital.

Dr. Main examined Mr. Goforth and said, "Goforth,

you say you are returning to Changte for work there. If you do, you will be committing suicide as surely as if you took an overdose of opium." This brought Mr. Goforth to his senses and from then on he became docile and obedient. The doctor's orders were that he should return to Canada as soon as possible.

Due to Jonathan's condition, arrangements were immediately made to return to Canada. Even during the trip home his illness did not hinder him from witnessing for His Master. He made a profound impression on many on board by his unbroken patience, cheerfulness, and unselfish regard for others, which characterized his whole demeanor and behavior. Upon arrival, the Goforths obtained a suitable home in Toronto, trusting the Lord to undertake for all the extra expense. He always proved faithful!

On this furlough we first became impressed with the way God had been raising up intercessors for us. Frequently one or more came up at the close of a meeting, saying they had prayed for us every day for years; some even from the time we had left for China. One day—not now—we shall know the "why" of many victories and perhaps too the "why" of many failures because someone had failed to "hold the ropes."

For years, the teaching which was called "higher criticism" and "modernism" had been increasingly taught in the colleges of the homeland, and its influence had become more and more evident on the foreign field. Mr. Goforth utterly refused to give his vote that both sides, fundamentalists and modernists, be allowed to preach and teach as they felt led. He cited the case of Hopinfu. There was but one thing for him to do—send in his resignation. The Home Board insisted he should remain a member of the North Honan mission of which he was the founder, but recommended that he be set entirely free from his Changte field to carry on the revival work to

which he felt called. His salary was to be continued, but
he himself would be responsible for his home and travel.

The question of where to make a home or rather,
headquarters, was a difficult one, as the future life was
to be nomadic. Several hundred miles south of Changte
was a beautiful plateau called Kikungshan. The climate
at this popular health resort was mild both winter and
summer. Since this place was central, and suitable for
residence at any season of the year, we decided to make
our home there.

During the following two years we "moved on" on an
average of every five days. The following are some extracts from a letter written to the home folks at this time
of a journey to South China:

"We made the journey of six days from Wuchow to
. . . Kweilin, by small house-boat. And it was small!
From our one possible seat, a board, I was able to run
the charcoal stove, cook all that was to be cooked, set
the table (a valise on board), and dip water out of the
river, without moving from my seat! . . .

"Jonathan does love to have a little fun and he cer-
tainly had it one day at my expense. Among the things
Mrs. Jaffray had packed in the hamper were a number
of what looked to us like small oranges. Jonathan peeled
one and took a good bite! I did not see his face at the
moment . . . So when he said, 'Just taste it,' I did—for
I am fond of *sweet* oranges—but oh, it was not an orange,
but a lime! . . .

"There were some real discomforts, such as the violent rocking of the boat passing over the *three hundred
and fifty rapids* en route; we could not get over the
seasick feeling this movement gave. Then we forgot to
bring candles or lamp, so were forced to either sit in
the dark on the board seat or get to the hard board bed
at six-thirty every evening. . . ."

A full schedule of meetings at mission stations along
the river routes, west of Canton, had been arranged for

Mr. Goforth. The same tokens of the Holy Spirit's presence and power were manifest at every place visited. His wife was unable to accompany him on this part of the tour owing to a somewhat serious breakdown. After some weeks in the Matilda Hospital, Hong Kong, she returned to Kikungshan where she found their new home nearing completion.

It was well on in the summer before Mr. Goforth returned from the south. Probably two hundred or more missionaries were then gathered on the hilltop. We had hoped Mr. Goforth might have two months of complete rest in the new home from which we could see a beautiful valley over a thousand feet below. For only a few brief days he was able to enjoy it all without a care. Then the urgent request came to lead a series of meetings on the hilltop for the missionaries. Though longing for rest, he could not refuse.

Almost immediately after the meetings for missionaries, an invitation came from General Feng Yuhsiang for Mr. Goforth and his wife to hold meetings among his soldiers. The General and his army were three days south of the Yangtse River in an extremely hot region. When the invitation came, word had just been received of cholera raging on the plains. Mr. Goforth never for a moment hesitated in responding to the General's call, but his weaker partner did shrink from facing the heat and cholera. Two other ladies promised if I decided to take the risk they would go with me.

The evening had come when a decision must be made. Opening my Bible in a rambling way, my eye lit on these words: "He that observeth the wind shall not sow and he that regardeth the clouds shall not reap" (Ecclesiastes 11:4). The following morning *we* were en route to Marshal Feng's army.

When we arrived four days later, General Feng came to see us an hour after our arrival. He was over six feet tall, and every inch a General. His manner was a curious and striking mixture of humility, dignity, and quiet power.

Twice every day Dr. Goforth had an attentive audience of one thousand men, chiefly officers. Most of the women's meetings were separate, when God gave me much help in speaking to them. At our last meeting, practically all the officers' wives present said they wished to follow the Lord Jesus.

At one of the last meetings for the men, General Feng broke down as he tried to pray. What seemed to affect him was the thought of his country. As soon as he could recover from his sobs, he stood up, and facing his officers, pleaded with them to think and work and pray for their country. One of his staff officers followed, praying earnestly, then one after another of the officers, with sobs and tears, cried to God on behalf of themselves and their country.

The worst famine in the annals of China faced the people of North-Central China in the late summer of 1920. Thirty to forty million people faced starvation. Famine reports coming from Changte were heart-rending and too horrible to publish. The whole Changte staff gave themselves over to meet the unparalleled crisis.

The writer, forced to remain at the Kikungshan mountain home, gave herself as steward for famine funds. During the winter of 1920–21 over $120,000 passed through her hands to various famine relief centers.

Some months later our Changte friends wanted us to lead a campaign of evangelism through the Changte field, as people's hearts had been wonderfully opened through their relief work. A band of eight picked evangelists and two Bible women were to accompany us, for a very full campaign was planned. All, or most of the main stations throughout the entire Changte field were to be visited, one or two meetings a day for the Christians and the rest of the time to be given to aggressive evangelism for the heathen. Part of the band was to carry on preaching in villages while the main tent meetings were in progress. Then all would gather for the evening meeting.

All through those five months of physically hard labor—under which the health of the writer ultimately broke down—never once was Mr. Goforth heard to complain. When enduring the bitter cold of drafty tents and unheated rooms, hard brick beds, and often the torment from very small but very lively fleas, over forty of which met their fate at his hands early one morning—he remained calm and unperturbed.

The following is from a diary kept during this tour:

"We hear that about forty families have taken down their gods in the last place . . . large attractive gospel texts are given to each one destroying their household gods. These are put up where the main god had been. . . .

"A truly wonderful movement is going on among the teacher class of this region. It began several years ago while we were holding tent meetings here. It has now spread till a large number of government school-teachers in this county, with the city of Tzushien as its center, are now Christians."

"On arriving here, when Dr. Goforth saw the meeting-tent, he at once said, 'Why, you have made it far too large. It will hold six or seven hundred!' 'No, no, Pastor,' replied the Christians, 'wait and see if we won't have to raise the back part to accommodate more,' and they were right. . . ."

One evening, as we were having supper in our "mud hut," who should shyly make his appearance but a lad who had professed Christ that day, followed by another boy. "Pastor," he said, "this is my cousin. He too wants to be a Christian." Later, as the boys left, my husband's face glowed with joy. "Truly this is a work that angels might covet!" he exclaimed. Three thousand publicly confessed Christ during this tour.

Following the winter of reaping on the famine fields at Changte, the Goforths made their second visit to South China. On this tour Mr. Goforth saw blessed signs of the Holy Spirit's convicting and transforming power at each center visited.

The following testimony to the importance of memorizing the Word of God, written about this time, was found among Dr. Goforth's papers:

"It is well to be able to repeat Scripture, but it is of very great importance to remember where it is in the Bible. . . . My wife seems to regard me as her walking concordance and my Chinese fellow-workers seem to think that I know everything in the Bible, but I am ever wishing I could spend several hundred years at the Bible.

"Since the New Version of the New Testament came out in Chinese, I will in a few days have gone over it thirty-five times in the Chinese text, comparing it with the Authorized and Revised New Testaments. My method now is to go over each verse five times, but ever trying after the first time to repeat it from memory, and even though I am sure of the meaning, I still read for comparison both English versions."

Before he crossed the Borderland, he had read the Bible seventy-three times from cover to cover.

The following are extracts from Mr. Goforth's record of one period with Marshal Feng and his army:

"Less than eleven years ago, General Feng and all his men were heathen. Now, for its size, the army under General Feng is the greatest Christian army on earth. It is about thirteen months since we spent thirteen days in meetings with the army. On the last day we baptized nine hundred and sixty men. That same day, four thousand six hundred and six officers and men partook of Communion.

"A few days later, General Feng was promoted to Divisional Commander and sent to support the appointee to the military governorship of Shensi. A Chinese writing from the first city in the Province that the Christian army passed through, said: 'Other soldiers when they came seized our houses and public buildings and made off with anything they took a fancy to, and our wives and daughters were at their mercy, so that the people called them the soldiers of hell. Now General Feng leads his men through the city and nothing is disturbed and nothing is molested. Even the General lives in a tent, as his men do, and everything they need they buy, and no one is abused. The people are so delighted the people call them the soldiers of heaven. . . .'

". . . Kaifeng for centuries has been notorious as a city of stagnant ponds. Now the Christian Governor is about to drain them off into a river to the south. All women of ill repute have been sent from the city. If the Governor remains long enough in the Province he will open a reformatory to reclaim such unfortunates. . . .

". . . In accord with the Governor's [General Feng's] request, we are planning to give all October to special evangelistic effort at Kaifeng. After supper we went out to inspect a couple of theater buildings, to see if they could be used for the coming meetings, and if they prove unsuitable, the Governor says he will erect an auditorium to seat several thousands. . . .

". . . The Governor is as zealous for the living God as was Nehemiah. Will the Canadian Presbyterian Church stand by him and cheer him on by adequately striving to save her part of the Province? At this time of times the Foreign Mission Board is faced with a staggering deficit of $166,000, and rumors of retrenchment are reaching us. What! Retrench? When such an open door invites us? The deficit is staggering, but that sum would not pay the tobacco bill of Presbyterians for one month! But why a deficit at all? . . . our annual gifts to save fourteen millions of heathen are . . . so vast a sum that it would hardly keep the ladies of the Canadian Presbyterian church in face powder for a year! Are we not insulting Him who paid our debt on Calvary? . . ."

A full year passed in work among the soldiers in General Feng's army, during which time over four thousand of the soldiers were baptized. Then Dr. Goforth received an urgent call from his old field of Changte, again to lead a campaign of tent evangelism through the field as before. Dr. Goforth hesitated. He had promised the Christian General to give the rest of his time till furlough to the soldiers, but the call of his old field was the call of his first love. He laid the matter before the General, who, on hearing the whole matter, generously set my husband free to spend the winter before furlough in leading this campaign in Honan.

Dr. Goforth no longer had his wife to take care of him, as she had been forced to return to Canada in broken health.

In every place souls were being saved. In one place Dr. Goforth mentions seventy having taken a stand, in another over one hundred. At the close of one of his last letters he wrote: "I am sixty-five today . . . *Oh, how I covet, more than a miser does his gold, twenty more years of this soul-saving work.*" Immediately at the close of this blessedly fruitful tour, Dr. Goforth left China for furlough.

On the steamer crossing the Pacific were two ladies. One was Miss Rollier, a French lady and an Indo-China missionary. The other was Madam Karinski, a former prima donna of the Russian court, upon whose head a price had been set by the Soviet government. This Russian lady was in great distress. Her outlook financially was hopeless; spiritually, the foundations of what faith she had seemed sinking from under her.

Miss Rollier begged Dr. Goforth to help this distressed woman. For several days, passengers pacing the deck witnessed a remarkable scene. The three sat side by side, Mr. Goforth in the center with his English Bible, Miss Rollier with her French Bible, and Madam with her Russian Bible. Each difficulty of this poor woman, each question of faith, Dr. Goforth met with a passage of Scripture, Miss Rollier acting as interpreter. On the third day she exclaimed, "I see it all now. Praise the Lord! I must tell the good news to my people!" She had been urged by some theatrical men on board from New York to sign a contract to sing for them. At once she gave up all thought of that life and joined the missionary party.

One of Mr. Goforth's most lovable traits was his simple humanness. On this journey, with great zest he joined children or older ones in deck hockey and shuffle-board. Though an opportunity to engage in outdoor sports came his way but rarely, when it did, he entered into the game with such joyous enthusiasm as to add to the pleasure of others. In this way he made many contacts with those who habitually avoided missionaries, with a testimony for his Master which flowed naturally.

12

GOD'S ROAD TO MANCHURIA

Where'er you ripened fields behold
Waving to God their sheaves of gold,
Be sure some corn of wheat has died,
Some saintly soul been crucified:
Someone has suffered, wept, and prayed,
And fought hell's legions undismayed.

A. S. Booth Clibborn

During this furlough, which began in the spring of 1924, Dr. Goforth's meetings numbered considerably over four hundred. He was now nearing his sixty-eighth year and feared being retired by his Board. It was therefore with the zeal and enthusiasm of a young man that he responded to the call of the Foreign Mission Board, commissioning him to return to China to find a field and found a new mission, the North Honan Mission having gone, as a Mission, into the Union.

He felt the need of a young co-worker, but unless he could get the right man, he was determined to go alone. God's man was Allan Reoch, a Knox College student. God seated Dr. Goforth next to Allan at a dinner and called Allan to China that evening.

The following story we give in Dr. Goforth's own words, as he delighted to tell it:

"One day, early in February, 1926, my wife, whose health had for some time been steadily declining, was resting on the sofa, waiting for the ambulance which was to take her to the Toronto General Hospital. Suddenly the doorbell rang, and the phone sounded simultaneously. The latter was to say the hospital was full and my wife would need to wait two or three days before a bed was vacant. The door call brought a cable from Marshal Feng in China, begging me to come at once. Reading the cable to my wife, I said, 'What shall I do? It is impossible for me to leave you as you are,' for we all thought she could not live many months. My wife, after covering her face for a moment, as if in prayer, looked up and said with decision, 'I'm going with you.' The Board was meeting at the time, so I laid before them Marshal Feng's cable and they heartily agreed to my going at once, but, when I said my wife would accompany me, they looked aghast and said that was impossible, for she would die on the way. I replied to this, 'You don't know that woman as well as I do. When she says she is going, she will go!' So they gave in."

The year we now entered proved to be the most prolonged period of unbroken testing in sickness, separation and repeated disappointments the Goforths ever experienced. The first disappointment came when Dr. Goforth proposed to the China Inland Mission that the "Anwei Field" be handed over to our Church; this was considered by them as quite impossible. On hearing this, Dr. Goforth, being most anxious to reach Marshal Feng's army, made arrangements to leave at once for their home in Kikungshan. Here Mr. Reoch began intensive study of the language.

Dr. Goforth left immediately for Peking, but on ar-

riving there, to his great consternation, he found the
Marshal and his army had been forced beyond Peking,
northwestward, and the enemy were in control of the
capital. In the following six months, five times the door
opened into what seemed a promising field, but then
closed. All through these dark days, Dr. Goforth's faith
never wavered. Buoyantly happy and optimistic, he never
gave way for a moment to down-heartedness.

Soon he left in search of another field, little dreaming
he was never again to see the dear mountain home. Shortly
after he had gone, Communists forced the Goforth party
and all the other missionaries to evacuate the mountain.
Dr. Goforth joined us in Hsuchow for the journey to
Peking. His wife was carried into the hospital.

A few days later, Dr. Goforth received a letter from
the Irish Presbyterian Mission, Newchwang, Manchuria,
urging him to come to Manchuria. They wrote of three
possible fields. Dr. Goforth was very eager to start for
Manchuria at once, but his wife was so sick in the hospital
he was obliged to wait a week before the doctors gave
their consent for him to leave. But the lowest ebb had
been reached, and the long two years' fight back to health
had begun.

In January 1927, Dr. Goforth returned from a quick
survey trip to Manchuria, full of enthusiasm. He gathered our little band together and we started for Manchuria by train—and what a weak band we were! The leader,
an old man nearing seventy, with a semi-invalid wife; a
"Salvation Army lassie"—Miss Graham, from New Zea-
land; a Dutch lady—Miss Annie Kok; and Rev. Allan
Reoch, as yet struggling with the language.

Our train reached Changchun on one of the bitterest,
cold, stormy days of our long experience, either in Manchuria or Canada. As we drove through wide, *clean*
streets, between well-built foreign-looking houses, and
over excellent roads in an open "drosky" (a Russian car-

riage) we simply marvelled. So utterly unlike was it to the unsanitary, narrow, rough streets we had been accustomed to.

The field given to us comprised a vast territory reaching westward from the South Manchurian Railway like a fan two-thirds open. Only about thirty miles actually touched the railway, the field gradually increasing in width westward to Mongolia, and on northwest to Russia, a distance of almost four hundred miles.

With the overthrow of the Manchu dynasty, a marvelous tide of emigrants had begun trekking northward, past the Great Wall into the land of new hopes—Manchuria. In 1926, the year before we entered Manchuria, this human tide had reached into the millions. All through our region, villages and towns had begun to spring up like mushrooms. Then came the railways. The first of these junctioned the South Manchurian Railway at the city of Szepingkai and ran right through our field in a semi-circular fashion. This railway was completed only a few months before we entered the field. A second strategic railway was completed the following year, and a third, opening up the farthest northwest region, was commenced a little later. Missionaries had never resided in any part of that whole region. When we heard these things we could not but explain, "Truly the Lord's hand has been guiding us!" With such an open door before us, Allen Reoch left immediately for Szepingkai. For three months, we women waited at Changchun for Mr. Reoch to find suitable living quarters for us, while Dr. Goforth used this time of waiting for holding missions in Harbin and elsewhere.

Then a time of real testing came. China to the south of us was in a state of indescribable confusion and chaos. Hundreds of missionaries were being recalled from all parts of the country and many were being sent back to the Homeland; among these were our daughter and her husband and child. Then a message came from our British counsel in Mukden, ordering all British subjects to be ready to flee at a moment's notice, so we began living with valises packed.

At this juncture a letter came from Mr. Reoch, telling of an ideal place on one of the main streets of Szepingkai, suited for both residence and preaching-hall. We could obtain it but the rent was excessively high and the landlord demanded payment a year in advance. Mr. Reoch asked that word be sent back immediately by telegraph as to whether he should rent or not, lest we lose the chance.

If we gave Mr. Reoch permission to rent, word might come at any moment from the British Consul, forcing us to flee, which would mean roping our Board into heavy expense for nothing. Our little band, Miss Kok, Miss Graham, Dr. Goforth and myself, together sought for definite guidance, but no light came that night. All went to bed hoping that by morning we could see things clearly. At breakfast, Miss Graham with shining face opened her Bible and read the following verse: "He that observeth the wind shall not sow, and he that regardeth the clouds shall not reap" (Eccles. 11:4). A telegram was sent to Mr. Reoch to secure the property and we never heard any further word from the Consul!

Again we saw God's guiding and preventing hand over us, for every one of the five fields which had opened and then closed to us had been evacuated of all missionaries. On April 28, 1927, we moved into Szepingkai and took possession of our "promised land."

The following letter written by Dr. Goforth just five weeks after coming to Szepingkai tells something of how God set His seal of blessing upon the work from the very outset:

"We moved in on the twenty-eighth of April and commenced on Sunday, May first. Since then the preaching of the Word has gone on for three hours in the forenoon, and four in the afternoon. We have never been without hearers, and if our force of workers were only larger we could add to the preaching hours. From the very first day men began to turn to the Lord, sometimes more than a dozen during the day. You can imagine our joy at seeing about *two hundred decisions during the month of May*. . . .

"No one can escape the fact that the harvest to be gathered in the newest mission field of the Presbyterian Church in Canada is very great. The preachers at present taking part in the preaching here day by day are Mr. Su, my very able personal evangelist; a Mr. Cheng, whom the Scotch Mission has loaned to us for a time; Miss Graham and Miss Kok, my wife and myself. But what are these among so many? We haven't the shadow of a doubt but that the results we have seen here during May might have been seen in dozens of other centers in our new field had it been possible for our little band to be in other centers at the same time. *We plan for no big schools, no big hospitals, until the converted Chinese build and equip them, but we do plan to evangelize intensively.*

". . .In the western part of our field lives one of the . . . Mongol tribes. It will be our privilege and duty to carry the gospel to them also."

Just as soon as it had become certain the field of which I have been writing was to be given over to us, Dr. Goforth sent a full description of it to the Board, ending his letter with an earnest appeal for recruits. In the meantime, at Szepingkai, our little band met twice daily in the "Cozy Nook" over the chapel, for prayer. The burden on each one was how to evangelize the vast unreached field for which, as a mission, we were now responsible. Dr. Goforth, in his glowing optimism, fully expected the Board, and the Church behind it, to respond generously with men and money when they came to know of the field he had obtained.

But alas, when Dr. Grant's letter came, it made only too plain that we could not hope for the generous backing which Dr. Goforth had been anticipating. "No recruits for an indefinite period,"—"necessary to keep within your budget apportionment." Dr. Goforth's disappointment was crushingly great.

It seemed as if every human prop was being removed from under us. To remain at the door of the great region of untouched millions and to leave them to perish, Jonathan Goforth could not and would not stand for. One day, after a time of intense prayerful waiting on God for light, as we rose from our knees, Dr. Goforth drew himself up and with passionate earnestness exclaimed: "Our home Church has failed us; but the God of Hudson Taylor is ours. He will not fail us if we look to Him. *This field must be evangelized* and it cannot be done with our present small force. If we cannot get Canadians as channels for the Gospel message, we must get Chinese." Thus the blow that seemed to threaten the very existence of the new mission proved to be the blow that set Jonathan Goforth free.

In Shantung, North China, there was a very fine college and seminary for the training of young men and women as evangelists, of which Dr. Goforth's old and honored friend, Dr. John Hayes, was founder and principal. At once, Dr. Goforth sent a letter to Dr. Hayes, asking if he could send him some evangelists. About the same time this letter was written, Dr. Hayes had written and sent a letter to Dr. Goforth, saying that contending forces had swept over their whole region seven times, all churches were closed and Christian work was at a standstill. Consequently none of his graduating class had doors open to them. He closed his letter by saying, "*Could you use any of these men?*" At once, the message was sent, "Send us all you can."

Humbly, I must record that his "little faith" of a wife,

on hearing what he had written, exclaimed anxiously, "But Jonathan, they can't live on air—where is the money to come from for their support?" He replied, half sternly, half kindly, "Where is your faith? If God sends us men, He will send money for their support."

Some weeks passed before the first band of evangelists from Dr. Hayes arrived, and by that time we had received in *unsolicited* gifts sufficient funds to meet at least two months' salary for them. Dr. Goforth then said, "I see we have taken the right step in the right direction. I must send for more men."

As Mrs. Goforth was unable to undertake outside work, she was appointed secretary-treasurer of the "Evangelist Trust Fund."

Szepingkai had been for years an outstation of the Irish Mission, but until we moved in, no foreigners had resided there. Our coming was received with distinct suspicion, especially by the Japanese. Almost daily, Dr. Goforth received visits from Japanese military officers who asked all sorts of questions, the answers carefully recorded. These visits were repeated with the same questions asked. Dr. Goforth, however, never lost patience. After this had been going on for five weeks, the Japanese, without warning, closed our preaching hall. Dr. Goforth appealed to the British Minister in Mukden, who advised us all to go for a few weeks to Peitaiho, the seaside summer resort, and while we were absent, he would have the matter looked into.

We all had a delightful and helpful holiday by the sea, returning to Szepingkai in August, having received word from the British Minister that all had been arranged satisfactorily with the Japanese. From that time we had no more serious trouble, though the visits of the military continued several times a month.

The latter part of September, Dr. Goforth, Mr. Reoch, and three evangelists made a tour of the field. The fol-

lowing are a few brief extracts from Dr. Goforth's account
of that trip as sent to the Board:

> "We all travelled third class. It almost seemed that
> we were conducting an evangelistic campaign on wheels
> for the testimony to the grace of God was almost con-
> tinuous. On the day going up to Taonan, the conductor
> and others of the train crew invited me to go to the first-
> class carriage where it would be quieter and tell them
> of this salvation. I took one of the evangelists along. We
> both talked to them and the conductor and five or six
> others decided to serve the Lord Jesus Christ. Through
> the preaching going on at Szepingkai these months,
> dozens of the railway men have decided to serve the
> Lord.
>
> ". . . There is but one evangelist along three hundred
> and fifty miles of rail. He is stationed at Taonan, a city
> of perhaps one hundred thousand people. We were told
> six years had passed since a missionary had visited that
> city. Along the railway north and south from Taonan are
> six other cities with populations running from ten to
> forty thousand and as many more cities are from ten to
> twenty thousand off from the railway, and all these with-
> out even one evangelist. Indeed, you might go for over
> one hundred miles east of Taonan and a thousand miles
> west and never find an evangelist. . . ."

On the above trip, Dr. Goforth was taken ill. Leaving
the rest to complete the tour, he hastened home arriving
about five o'clock in the evening with a high fever and
heavy chill. By about eight o'clock, he became delirious.
Mr. Reoch returned at ten o'clock, and after consultation,
we decided if Dr. Goforth was no better by eleven-thirty,
Mr. Reoch would take the midnight train to Mukden and
return if possible with a doctor. I then went to my husband's bedside and stood there quietly praying the Lord
to undertake for us. As I prayed, his restlessness ceased,
and turning on one side, he fell into a sound sleep. At
eleven-thirty, he seemed quite cool. The fever was gone,

and he was still sleeping quietly. After a restful night, Dr. Goforth insisted on getting up and seemed quite himself.

Dr. Goforth was a firm believer in D. L. Moody's axiom that "it is better to get ten men to work, than to do the work of ten men." Just as soon as the preaching-hall work at Szepingkai was in good running shape with Miss Graham in charge, assisted by several evangelists, he decided to devote two weeks to Tungliao, an important center in the southwestern section of the field on the newly built railway.

We had had very little mail since leaving Szepingkai, so we were not aware of the fact that the dreaded plague had broken out in a region only a few miles west of Tungliao. The first word of this came to us in a letter from Mr. Reoch informing us of the deputation from Canada having reached Korea. They requested that we all meet them there as the news of the rapid spread of the plague in Manchuria was so alarming it was thought best that they remain in Korea.

We packed up at once and started. It was a bitterly cold day and the train was not heated. On this trip God delivered us from death when our train derailed and we unknowingly spent hours in a room full of plague victims. One third of Tungliao's population died of plague that winter.

On our return from Korea, we were right into the long, intensely cold Manchurian winter. Yet this very extreme cold helped to keep up the preaching-hall audiences. Dr. Goforth felt it was money well spent to keep a good fire going in the preaching hall downstairs. Carters passing the door half-perishing with cold, would stop, come in, and get warm and so hear the Gospel of the grace of God for the first time. One day, from my seat at the organ, I counted two hundred people pass the door in seven minutes. Dr. Goforth, though speaking usually only twice daily, spent many hours each day in the hall. The benefit of this to the work was twofold—his presence helped to attract the people, and by listening to the evangelists, he was able later to correct or suggest as need be. Newcomer evangelists soon learned that only soul-saving messages would be favored by the old pastor. All loved Dr. Goforth so much, none seemed to resent his quiet, gentle, guiding hand. The early half-hour for prayer and a brief message, each morning from eight to eight-thirty, was taken in turn by all the workers. Dr. Goforth always attended, and it was a time of helpful fellowship.

At the early approach of spring, and with an increased staff of evangelists, Dr. Goforth felt the time had come for the opening of Taonan, the city next to Szepingkai in strategic importance. It must be confessed that to take this advance step was quite contrary to the Home Board's orders, for as yet they had not even officially accepted the field. Dr. Goforth's position at this time was by no means an easy one. He fully realized his age limitations as he had already entered his seventieth year, but this fact, instead of causing him to "slow down," seemed to intensify the urge within him to press forward.

So to the opening of Taonan, Jonathan Goforth gave himself in his characteristic, whole-hearted way. Miss Graham, whose years in the Salvation Army had given her a unique power in preaching to men, was put in charge of the preaching-hall work at Szepingkai, while Miss Kok gave herself to the women's work for which she was equally well-fitted. A band of fine, consecrated evangelists remained to help Miss Graham, for the preaching was kept going seven hours a day.

Our first morning in Taonan, we inspected the buildings, which were just rooms side by side in the shape of an "L." The lower, shorter end faced the busy street. We were very shocked to find that every door and window frame and other inside woodwork had been wrenched away and carried off. This, we were told, was the custom at Taonan when property changed hands.

We concentrated all our attention first on fixing up a large room facing the street for a preaching hall. Here, as at Szepingkai, illuminated texts, pictures, hymn-scrolls, and an organ transformed the place into a beautiful room for the preaching of the gospel. An order for fifty benches had been given to a local carpenter and these now filled the hall. During those first two weeks after the hall was opened, four hundred had given their names as believing. Then came the problem of how to follow up and keep in touch with those who had taken this first step. One evangelist, therefore, was set apart for this follow-up ministry.

For years a promise to visit Vietnam for revival meetings had remained unfulfilled. Dr. Goforth decided to devote the summer months, which he might have claimed for his own holiday, for making this trip. It was indeed a wonderful experience. First came two weeks' meetings for the Alliance missionaries at their annual convention at Tourane. This was followed by days of blessing with the native preachers and workers at a place near Saigon.

A call had come for Dr. Goforth to give a series of revival talks to the missionaries gathered for the summer on Cheung Chau, an island near Hong Kong. Lack of space only keeps the writer from dwelling on this latter ministry. The affection and sympathy and the hearty response given to the messages remained as one of the most precious memories to both Dr. Goforth and his wife. The day we boarded our steamer for Shanghai, numbers of both missionaries and Chinese Christians came on board to see us off. We had not had an opportunity to see our cabin until they all had gone and the vessel was well on its way. Then, when we went below, we found the cabin filled with marvelous flowers!

On reaching our field in Manchuria we heard rumors of the dreaded plague having broken out again in the same region as the previous year. Day by day the news of its coming nearer and nearer was, to say the least, somewhat disturbing. The ninety-first Psalm came to mean much to us in those days. Plague-masks were generally worn and the report one day was that twenty-five had died one night in a section of Taonan. After this the plague gradually lessened, due to the efficient plague prevention measures carried out by the Japanese.

Dr. Goforth had planned to give the whole winter to Taonan, but God ordered otherwise. We had been there only a month when a letter came from the evangelist at Szepingkai, begging Dr. Goforth to return at once and take charge as Miss Graham had gone to open a work at Tungliao.

Thus, Mr. Reoch, who had little more than two very broken years at language study, and less than eighteen months of close touch with mission work, had to take over the charge of that great field. But he did not fail us nor his Divine Master.

13

TESTINGS AND TRIUMPHS

*When I attempt to do what I can't do, then I do
it in the power of the Spirit.*

G. Campbell Morgan

The winter of 1928–29 was very severe. Where the
Goforths lived above the chapel was scarcely ideal during
this cold weather. They had no shed, no storeroom, and
absolutely no place to keep things from freezing but in
their bedroom! Fortunately, it was a large room, and with
careful adjusting, was made into not only a bedroom, but
also a study and general sitting-room and store-room.
They had packed under their bedstead, among other
things, apples, eggs, oranges, canned milk, and anything
and everything that might be spoiled by freezing.

Dr. Goforth was urged by the Mukden doctors to have
his teeth extracted and so this was done by a Japanese
dentist. Returning to Szepingkai, we found our youngest
child, Fred, just arrived from Canada. His coming was
truly of the Lord. Dr. Goforth had caught cold in the
lower jaw and very serious complications followed. For
nearly four months, he was unable to go down even to

135

the chapel. He would not remain in bed, but rose as usual every morning.

For years Dr. Goforth had been asked to write about his revival experiences, but he could never get time. This illness was the opportunity for accomplishing this task. Day by day, Fred would sit at his typewriter and take down story after story from his father as he paced the floor. In the spring, Fred left us for Canada with the precious manuscript of *By My Spirit*.

Throughout the winter of 1929, while confined to those "upper rooms," Dr. Goforth directed the work of the Szepingkai field through the evangelists. The work throughout the entire field was growing rapidly. "Aggressive Evangelism" was the key-note of the work everywhere. Tent evangelistic campaigns during the warmer months were held at theaters or fairs or anywhere crowds could be reached. Shops, schools, prisons and homes were visited, tracts were given away and portions of Scriptures sold—this was all done besides the regular preaching-hall work.

For some time the matter of expense in getting evangelists from long distances had been greatly troubling Dr. Goforth and his co-workers. At the beginning of the work, when he had no Christian constituency to draw from, it was necessary. But now, some of our own Christians were coming forward, offering themselves for the work. There had been much prayer regarding this, but we had neither the staff nor the money to start a Bible-training school of our own.

It was, therefore, with great joy and relief that Dr. Goforth heard of a school being started in Newchang, Manchuria. Our young workers, after a time of testing on our own field, were sent for the three half-years' training, six months each year being given to the school work and six months to practical evangelism on the field.

Well over three years had now passed since Dr. Goforth took the step of faith for the supply of evangelists and money to support them. The workers had, during this time, increased from three to thirty, and as the staff increased, so did the donations for their support. *There was absolutely no soliciting of funds.*

The Mission had decided that we should return to Canada for furlough early in 1930, one reason for this being the writer was fast losing her sight from double cataract and at least one eye needed to be operated on.

The 1930–31 furlough was indeed a strange one. We experienced disappointment, even tragedy, on the one hand, but on the other, repeated mercies. The Goforths had an unforgettable tour, taking in among other places, Boston, New York, and Philadelphia, contacting supporters of our evangelists in Manchuria. Then came the operation for cataract on Mrs. Goforth's left eye which proved a complete success.

Word arrived that both Miss Graham and Miss Annie Kok had resigned. This was indeed serious news, seeing that our staff was so pitifully small. Little did we then realize that a still greater time of testing was at hand.

It had been decided, due to Mr. Reoch's urgent need for furlough, that we should hasten our return to Manchuria. On our farewell trip west Dr. Goforth's right eye began irritating, and we were forced to return to Toronto. During the following four months, Dr. Goforth went through operation after operation for dislodged retina of the right eye. Not till the latter part of April was all hope of restoring sight to that eye abandoned.

Miss Margaret Gay, an experienced nurse and a former worker in Honan, cancelled all her cases and gave herself to act as his night nurse. For months, with eyes bandaged, Dr. Goforth recounted to Miss Gay story after story as they later appeared in *Miracle Lives of China*, and Miss Gay took them down in shorthand. The book was actually in print before Dr. Goforth even saw the manuscript.

In the latter part of May, Dr. Goforth and his wife, accompanied by their son, Paul, left for Manchuria. Upon our return, we found that the conditions under which we lived and worked in Manchuria were continuously affected by the changing political situation.

From our windows over the preaching-hall at Szepingkai we could see a sort of miniature Eiffel Tower, from the top of which searchlights were continuously covering the town—this to guard against attacks by the threatening hoards of bandits, sometimes over one thousand strong. Barbed wire entanglements surrounded a large part of the town, electrically charged at night. Wrecking of the railways was not uncommon. These are but a few indications of the disturbed conditions which continued for years throughout the field. When the "clouds" became very threatening, we lived for days with valises packed, though none of us ever had to leave. Through it all, the work went on. Not one of the ten preaching-halls throughout the field had to be closed. New centers were being opened, and promising young converts were offering themselves as evangelists.

The following letter written by our own son, Paul, September 8, 1932, gives a picture of the conditions at that time:

"When Pastor Chang wrote this week to say he could not come to Szepingkai on account of sickness in his home, I decided to take the rent money to Tungliao. Telling none of the Chinese about my financial plans, I left Szepingkai . . . with seven hundred dollars in ten dollar notes pinned into the pockets of a waistcoat which I wore under a khaki shirt. . . .

"I was shown the new electrically charged fence surrounding Tungliao to keep the bandits out. The main effect apparently had been to *keep them in*; and the

victims have been numerous dogs and pigs. Little brick
forts throughout the city indicate that street battles with
the bandits are part of the regular program. Pastor Chang
says that all Tungliao was governed by bandits from
October, 1931, to January, 1932. In the magnificent railway station and its outbuildings, I looked in vain for a
single door or window which the vandals had not
smashed—glass, woodwork, and all. The station safe, a
bulky one, is still lying where they left it in the open—
upside down, door ripped off its hinges, and empty."

From the starting of the Manchurian Mission, the
attitude of the Home Board was "retrench," owing to the
Church's financial condition, while Dr. Goforth and his
co-workers were ever for "advance." At last, early in January of 1932, Dr. Goforth felt he must make his position,
once for all, clear to the Board. This he did in the following letter to our foreign mission secretary:

> ". . . as long as the Lord of the Harvest gives me
> strength I dare not stand still, but must extend the
> work. It may be questioned whether any other portion
> of God's earth so strongly invites to a forward evange-
> listic effort as does this Manchurian field. No matter
> how the work expands on present lines, the Home
> Church is not responsible for a single school, a single
> hospital, a single house, or a foot of land. All the build-
> ings are rented, and the year we cease to pay the rent
> they revert to the owners. Up to the present all evan-
> gelists used are paid by funds not raised by the Home
> Church, and they are clearly told that when the funds
> fail they return home. Even we missionaries can be
> recalled when the Home Church considers her obli-
> gation to evangelize this great perishing multitude of
> Chinese Mongols has ceased. But we think better of
> the Home Church than this. . . ."

The first six months of 1932 were given to continuous
and strenuous revival missions in the main centers
throughout the whole field. Then Dr. Goforth and his

wife had the most delightfully quiet, refreshing holiday of their life, by the sea at Peitaiho, the most beautiful summer resort of the Far East. Each evening toward sundown, the seventy-three-year-old missionary and his not so young wife sat together on the west veranda, drinking in the marvelous beauty of the scene before them. The wide, deep valley, stretched far westward to the mountain ranges beyond, and the sunsets had an indescribable coloring and changing glory! Later, Dr. Goforth recalled with deepest gratitude to God that he have been given such a rich feast of vision to remember when physical darkness came.

Dr. Goforth escaped from taking what might easily have been a fatal step. We had taken passage on a Japanese boat from Darien to Tangku on the mainland of China. We had often been on boats where a narrow passageway led from one side of the boat to the other, connecting the two decks. It was evening when we boarded the vessel. Dr. Goforth opened a door, leading as it seemed to him, across the passage to the other deck. He had taken one step and had actually raised a foot for the next, when a hand seemed laid upon him, pressing him back against the door, which had sprung to. At first he thought that he had met somebody, but on looking closely, he discovered that it was not a through passage, but steep steps leading down to the lower deck. The walls on either side were straight, with no banisters, and had he taken that step, he would undoubtedly have been thrown headlong to the foot of the stairs. When he came to me, his face was quite white, and he said, "Rose, the Lord has delivered me again!"

When we returned from our holidays, a warm invitation came from the missionaries and Christians of the old Changte field to visit them and to hold a week's meetings. A tent which had been erected for the meetings and which held from eight hundred to a thousand people, was filled several times a day. We met with many of our beloved children in Christ. But time had wrought great changes—many loved faces were missing. The little treed-in corner of the compound, with our three precious mounds was fast filling. Many times later, we both praised God for allowing us to have that last visit to the dear old station with many unforgettable memories.

The evening of March 30, 1933, Dr. Goforth walked in gropingly to where I was sitting; he was very pale. Then he said quietly, almost in a whisper, "I fear the retina of my left eye has become dislodged." Dr. Goforth and his wife then made the long journey to Peking, where for four months he went through, almost daily, the same terrible ordeal he had suffered in Toronto two years before, but to no avail. Not once did he question or complain because of his blindness.

We had not been in Peking long when letters from the field began to cause Dr. Goforth great uneasiness. About the beginning of July, we went to Dairen, on the southern coast of Manchuria to seek help from a Japanese doctor. Word reached us here of the Home Board's drastic cut in allowance for general Mission expenses. How drastic was the cut may be seen when only eight dollars was to be allowed per month for all general mission expenses for Szepingkai, and its fourteen outstations, and the same amount for the whole Taonan field. The work could not be carried on; evangelists were being dismissed.

It was probably the most serious situation Dr. Goforth had ever faced, yet he exclaimed, "The devil is trying his best to wreck our mission, but God is with us and He will bring us through!"

On reaching Szepingkai, a general meeting of missionaries, Chinese workers and leaders, was called to face the crisis. Some of the evangelists who had been dis-

missed were restored, but others who had not proved
satisfactory were not taken back. Our evangelists now
numbered almost seventy. Then reports began to arrive
from all sections of the field indicating that the spirit of
self-support seemed to have settled down upon the
Christians everywhere. Even small groups began to vie
with one another in putting up their own church buildings and undertaking all running expenses of their center.

We managed to face this crisis due to the willing spirit
of self-support which the Christians showed at this time.
Also, a very sobering letter to the Home Board alerted
them to the great necessity of continuing this great evangelistic work which was harvesting many souls for the
Master. In response, the Home Board cabled us a large
donation immediately.

The definite advance made at this time may be seen
from the following brief comparative statistics:

Adult baptisms, 1932, 472:   Givings of Christians, $ 4,312.12
Adult baptisms, 1933, 778:   Givings of Christians,   8,285.05
Adult baptisms, 1934, 966:   Givings of Christians, 14,065.98

The first need as Dr. Goforth faced blindness was for
a Chinese companion. It was a problem to find just the
right man for such a position. We prayed much about it.

Before leaving Dairen, we decided the companion
should not be paid from the evangelists' fund, so we would
need to pray for a donation which could be used for his
support. On reaching Szepingkai, a letter awaited us from
a gentleman in New York enclosing a check sufficient for
one year's salary. The letter said, "This is for Dr. Goforth,
to help in any way because of his loss of sight." So we
had the year's salary in hand one week before Mr. Kào
came, a young man perfectly suited for the job.

When Dr. Goforth faced inevitable blindness, for a
very brief season, he feared his ministry for the Lord had
come to an end. Most of his public preaching to heathen

audiences had to be given up, but not personal interviews. His wonderful knowledge of the text of Scripture enabled him to deal with seekers, for he could tell them where to find a passage needed.

One of Mr. Kao's chief duties was to read the Chinese Bible aloud to Dr. Goforth. Sometimes, as he read very quickly, a character would be overlooked or miscalled. To his astonishment, Dr. Goforth would detect the error and quietly check him up, so familiar had the Chinese text become.

How we wish it were possible to give several chapters to the personal stories of men and women who have been led out of darkness "into His marvelous light"! The following are but brief outlines of a few Dr. Goforth enjoyed recounting later when in Canada:

The poorest Christian in the Tungliao church, a swineherd, on hearing Pastor Chang's plea for funds to purchase a plot of ground on which to build their own church, came forward saying, "Pastor, I want to help, but I have only my pigs. The Lord Jesus has done so much for me, I must do my part. Tell me, what can I do?" The Pastor knew the desperate poverty of the poor fellow. The most he could get to live on probably would not exceed two or three dollars a month. All he could say was, "Ask the Lord to show you." As the man turned away, he thought, *I cannot give the Lord anything but my best.* Going to where his pigs were, he picked out the fattest and finest and drove it to the market where he sold it for thirteen dollars and thirty-five cents; perhaps he never had seen so many silver dollars at one time. But as he counted out the thirty-five cents, he said to himself, *I can't give the Lord a broken dollar!* Somehow he made up the amount to fourteen dollars and brought them to the Pastor as his share in getting their own church. Is it any wonder, with such an example, that within a year not only the land was secured, but a simple and suitable church building erected free of debt? Better still, before another year had passed, the building had to be enlarged and since that time has been enlarged a second time.

A true miracle of grace was Mr. Tung of Fanchiatun, an important center north of Szepingkai. Baptized thirty years before, he had for many years been a backslider, living deep in sin; drink, opium, gambling, etc., all of which had gained a strangle-hold upon him. Through one of our Christians, he was persuaded to attend revival meetings at Szepingkai, where he and his family were lodged in the Goforth's guest-room. He became awakened, convicted, and before leaving, was literally "a new man in Christ Jesus." Returning home, he at once set himself to win others to Christ and became the leader in one of the most remarkable Christian movements we have yet seen. When visiting his center six months later, it took almost two hours for the members of the forty families he had won as believers, to pass before us in single file, each one being introduced to us by Mr. Tung. A street on which all the houses had been owned by Mr. Tung, was named "Harlot Alley." After these houses had been cleaned out and only Christians allowed to live in them, the street was renamed, "Heaven's Grace Alley."

Many a Sunday-school in the homeland has been thrilled with the story of the two Sun girls. When the alarm came that bandits were at the front gate, all the family managed to escape, but two girls of about twelve and fourteen. The younger hid in an inner room, but the elder stood in the center of the main room, quietly praying as the bandits rushed in. While many of them began looting, the leader seized the girl by the throat, threatening to choke her if she did not tell where her father had hidden. "I don't know," she said. He then tightened his grip so that she was indeed nearly choked, saying, "You lie!" She replied, "I am a Christian," and then with a sudden inspiration, she said, "I think you would like me to sing." At this the men stopped looting and shouted for her to sing to them. Calmly she sang a verse of "Jesus Loves Me." They were all so delighted that they called for more. She said, "My cousin sings better than I do, I'll call her." When the child who had hidden appeared, the two sang together the second verse of "Jesus Loves Me." Then the bandit leader called to the others to stop looting and to bring back everything that had been taken away. Putting into the children's hands two dollars, he shouted to the men to leave. They made off without doing any further harm. When this story was told me by one of the girls, I asked her, "Did you not feel greatly terrified when the bandits were all about you?" "Oh, no!" she replied, "I knew the Lord was with me."

SUNSET

We have all eternity to tell of victories won for Christ, but we have only a few hours before sunset to win them.

Anon.

Early in January, 1934, the Mission Council met at Szepingkai and all were encouraged by the reports received from every section of the field. This was in spite of an ever present political menace since most of our field was in the very center of the troubled area.

Wonderful stories were told indicating God's care of all of us. Two of our missionaries had planned to start from Szepingkai for Taonan on a certain day. Without any apparent reason, they changed their plan and left a day earlier. The train they originally planned to travel by was wrecked by bandits tearing up the track, and while wholesale looting was in progress, a freight train going at full speed ran into the wreck and over two hundred were killed or injured.

Immediately after Council, Dr. Goforth started a full campaign of revival missions throughout the field. The first center he visited was Tungliao with zero weather, packed audiences, and an epidemic of flu raging! Dr. Goforth's voice was often drowned by the coughing. He contracted the flu, or whatever the epidemic was. How I begged him to give in and be nursed, and even let me take his meetings, for I could see he was really ill! But no, he never missed a meeting. He was very quiet but very pale and seemed all through these days—indeed, through the next three months—like a man gropingly taking one step at a time, and doubtless he was.

For many weeks that winter, what I have just described was repeated at other centers. But God's servant was paying a price. Racked with coughing, sometimes he would stand holding to the desk till the attack passed, and then go on with his message. This went on all through the winter till April when we returned home to Szepingkai. Then the collapse which all had been fearing for months came. One morning, he arose intending to go for a day's preaching, but he became so deathly faint, he yielded to my urging that he return to bed. "Have you any pain?" I asked. "Yes," he replied, "very severe under my left shoulder." "How long have you had it?" "Three days." "Why didn't you tell me before?" "Because I was afraid if you knew, you would keep me from my work!"

Not an instant of time was lost. Warm compresses, inhalations, and everything I could possibly think of to do, I did. After four hours a Japanese doctor came and his diagnosis: aborted pneumonia. So the acuteness of the attack was checked, but in the days that followed, Mr. Reoch and I were in despair for Dr. Goforth insisted on the Chinese being allowed to see him. In they flocked, and between his violent attacks of coughing, he entertained with a cheerful, smiling face, the Christians who would not be kept from him nor he from them. So to save him from himself, it was decided I should take him at once to the seaside. Pastor Su was also in very poor health, so with the two invalids, and Mr. Kao, the companion, and one servant, we started for the seaside.

For weeks Dr. Goforth rested by the sea. His great weakness and incessant coughing with slight hemorrhages gave great concern. At the beginning of June, one lung became affected and in a few weeks, the other lung also. I had sent word of Dr. Goforth's condition to many friends, asking for prayer. About the middle of July, or perhaps a little later, I noticed a very marked change coming over my husband. His temperature became normal, his old strength and vigor returned.

Toward the end of July two visiting doctors gave Dr. Goforth a clean bill of health. Three days later we were en route for Szepingkai! Among the many letters awaiting us on our arrival "home" was one from a prominent Presbyterian minister in Toronto. It said in part:

> ". . . I have a growing conviction, and I believe it is of the Lord, that you ought to return home and spend a few years in the homeland before your call comes for higher service. I very well understand that you will feel that you ought to stay at the post of duty up to the very end—but have you ever thought that God may be demanding the greater sacrifice of coming home and out of your ripe experience, rekindle the fires of missionary zeal that are, I assure you, on the decline in the Home Church. . . . I believe we need you, the Church needs you to arouse it."

Not long after, the above letter was followed by another, also from a leading minister in Canada. The gist of it was much the same in thought. To these, Dr. Goforth at first gave little attention, but went on as before—working to the limit of his strength. Then Mrs. Goforth's steady decline in health led them both to pray that the Lord might make it unmistakably clear as to whether they should remain or return home.

The writer's sudden and serious collapse in late 1934

resulted in the question as to whether or not we should
return to Canada being laid aside. The question, now,
was "how speedily arrangements could be made to get
the Goforths home."

Of the many farewell messages which reached us we
give but one—an extract from a farewell message from
the Reformed Presbyterian Mission, Manchuria:

> "Our acquaintance with Dr. Goforth goes back to
> the days of fellowship and blessing through the Holy
> Spirit's presence and power in the far South. . . . He
> lived in the Holy Spirit's presence so that no power on
> earth could shake his confidence.
>
> "In the meetings he seemed like a man who was
> clearing the track for a powerful locomotive that was
> waiting only for a clear track and that would not come
> until the track was clear. He was as sure of the Spirit
> as of tomorrow's sun, and just as sure that only clouds
> of sin could obscure His glory."

For days before we were to leave, Christians came in
with most mysterious hints, but none would reveal what
was going on. Then came the farewell service. Though
Dr. Goforth could not see, many eagerly told him of the
beautiful banners, silk, satin and velvet, which covered
the entire walls of both men's and women's sections of
the chapel. On a long table in front of the preacher's desk
were twelve beautiful silver shields, each engraved with
a message such as: "Faithful Servant of Jesus Christ" and
"A True Pastor Leaves Love Behind." But that which
called forth the greatest admiration from Chinese and
missionaries alike was a framed Chinese character for
"love." It was worked in delicate colors on white satin in
Shanghai embroidery and framed. This came as a personal gift to Dr. Goforth from a prominent Szepingkai
merchant whom God had used Dr. Goforth to lead out
from a very evil life into a life of fellowship with Christ.
There were other gifts, that from Pastor Su being espe-

cially touching. He had come to us alone with two gold rings. He said, "I want you always to keep these on your bodies to remind you of my devotion to you."

Three days later, the Szepingkai station platform was crowded with heartbroken Christians. I placed Dr. Goforth carefully in front of a large window and the crowd pressed together before it. Dr. Goforth, though unable to see them, kept gently bowing his head that they might know his heart was with them, his face turned upward at times, indicating the blessed hope of reunion. Mr. Kao was closest to the window and was the first to break down weeping. The others followed quickly and as the train began to move, that great crowd kept following, straining through tear-dimmed eyes to catch a last glimpse of their beloved Pastor.

The "Empress of Japan" had scarcely touched dock when Dr. Goforth was claimed for numerous meetings in Vancouver and his word was barely given for these when a telegram came from Dr. Grant, our Foreign Mission Secretary, saying "Come on by first train." Dr. Goforth replied, "Delayed by meetings." Then he set himself to face a full schedule for Vancouver and Victoria.

On reaching Toronto, two weeks later, he fully expected a stern rebuke from Dr. Grant for his disobedience, but the old secretary simply smiled as he warmly welcomed back the Church's missionary pioneer. Then it came out that Dr. Grant had been receiving such glowing reports of the Vancouver meetings he was more than glad Dr. Goforth had not obeyed his summons.

The Board prepared a heavy itinerary for Dr. Goforth to include the most strategic centers throughout Ontario and Quebec. The travelling was to be chiefly by car. The schedule, outside of travel, included an average of eight to ten meetings a week. Some, on hearing of this proposed itinerary, said, "It is simply suicidal for a seventy-

six-year-old man to attempt such a strain!" But Dr. Goforth did not hesitate for a moment. He rejoiced only
that doors were open to him. It was for him to enter them
and go through each day as it came, quietly, trustfully,
in the strength given him.

All through the journeyings up and down the country
in Ontario and elsewhere, Dr. Goforth never failed to
meet a scheduled appointment. There were times when
others could see he was all but exhausted after a long
journey, but no word was uttered by him as to how he
felt. I knew as no other that he simply went forward by
Divine empowering.

He gave forth his messages fearlessly with much of
the old fire of fifty years before. Many of his clerical
brethren did not see eye to eye with him and "some were
offended at the words which he spake." Yes, some—not
many—would not receive him in their pulpits. One whole
Presbytery actually closed their doors to him. Many times
as he went throughout the churches he remarked on the
blessed and powerful influence of the Women's Missionary Society. When inclined to be depressed at the general
deadness of the church, cheer and comfort would often
come from the warmth of receptions given by the women.

The last family Christmas Day reunion was a very
broken one. Of the six living children, only two, Mary
and Fred, were present. Toward the end of the evening,
a niece with her husband joined the party. The husband,
somewhat of a stranger, sat apart. He had at one time
been an earnest Christian, but had backslidden. Months
later, after Dr. Goforth had gone, the niece told Mrs.
Goforth the following: "My husband took little interest
in what was going on that evening, but kept watching Dr.
Goforth and what he saw in his face and actions brought
him back to his Lord. Since that evening he has been a
new man."

The early months of 1936 were spent in strenuous

itineraries through Ontario. As the time for the General
Assembly in June drew near, a great burden seemed to
come upon Dr. Goforth for a message which would awaken
the Church from its terrible lethargy. His Assembly address, his last, was listened to by dignitaries and leaders
with marked attention, but with no special signs of spiritual awakening.

A short time in a lake cottage followed the Assembly
and since no calls had come for summer conferences in
Canada, Dr. Goforth accepted invitations to conventions
in the United States. The first of these was at Keswick,
New Jersey, a most blessed ten days.

From Keswick, New Jersey, we travelled down to the
beautiful Southland, farther south than we had ever been,
to Asheville, North Carolina. After winding around sharp,
steep turns for some time, we came suddenly upon "Ben
Lippen," the site of the Convention, and what a welcome
awaited us!

As I attempt to recall that month spent among those
dear people on Ben Lippen, words simply fail me. Dr.
Goforth repeatedly spoke of it as "the crowning Conference of my life," though in saying this, he did not know
it was to be his last. Dr. McQuilkin, the beloved leader,
gave over to Dr. Goforth, as part of his work for the three
conferences that were to follow, the early morning prayer-
meeting from seven to eight. The attendance at these
morning meetings was exceptionally large—probably
four-fifths of the entire Conference.

One morning, I was rather late, and overtaking a lady,
I said, "Do you manage to get out to these early meetings?" She replied, "Oh, I never miss! It is at these meetings I get such a blessing. I'm too nervous to pray aloud,
so when the meeting is left open for prayer, I lean forward
and raise my head, keeping my eyes on Dr. Goforth's
face. It is from what I see there that my blessing comes.
He stands so still and is so calm and quiet and seems to

just radiate peace and joy and faith and hope—everything my heart craves for!"

The young people flocked about him. One day I laughingly told them, "You never give me a chance to get near my husband!" There were always two or more contending for the honor and favor of leading him.

All too soon, as it seemed, the time came for farewells. A number escorted us down the mountain to the railway station at Asheville.

On that first Sunday back in Toronto, a brief record was kept of how that day was spent, which I give here as it is at least revealing of one day in a missionary's life. At the time, the story we heard in England came to mind, of a business man, who on hearing how a missionary was being worked when in the homeland, said, "I think you people are inclined to say when missionaries return home—'Here's a missionary. Come, let us kill him!' "

"Sunday morning, at nine o'clock, Mr. and Mrs. A. arrived in their motor. We drove with them thirty miles to . . . ., where we were taken into the home of Mr. and Mrs. B. The A's left at once and for some time I endeavored to entertain our host and hostess as Jonathan was to have a busy day. By ten forty-five we were driven over to the church and handed over to the Rev. Mr. C., who had Jonathan address the Sunday-school and, later, the morning service, at the close of which Mr. C. drove us to the house of Mr. and Mrs. D. Dinner was late, so to be on time for the afternoon service we had to leave before we could finish. We were driven some miles to . . . . . . and handed over to the minister, Rev. Mr. E., who after the service, put us in charge of the F.'s, who took us to . . . ., where we had supper with Mr. and Mrs. G., after which we motored to . . . . . . for the evening service, after which we were given over to Mrs. H., with whom we were told we were to spend the night, though we had hoped to return to Toronto that evening.

The following day, Mrs. I. arrived some time after noon and motored us back to Toronto. Needless to say, we were glad to get home!"

I think it was the next Sunday, Dr. Goforth was to speak but once, and that an evening service. On rising he said, "Instead of going out this morning, let us have a feast of the Word. Read me that precious book, the Gospel of John." So that day, as he reclined, I read to him chapter after chapter, sixteen in all. We hoped to have finished the Gospel, but supper-time came, and he returned too late from the evening service to read more that night. Sometimes when I was reading to him, a slight slip was made, but quickly the correction would come from him. What a feast it was to him!

For long years Dr. Goforth had contended for putting aggressive evangelism *first*. He urged that any line of mission work, whether medical, educational, or any other kind, could only be justified when made means to the one great end—the propagation of the Gospel.

One day in that last week in Toronto, he had been reclining on the sofa, as usual, apparently thinking very keenly, when he called me to him. He rose, drew me down beside him and said, "I have been doing some mental figuring and the result is beyond what I expected. My dear, *I have demonstrated beyond any question of a doubt what just giving the gospel a chance will result in!* If all the missionaries in China in 1934, our last year in Manchuria, had had an equal number of converts per head, as our six missionaries, namely, one hundred and sixty-one per missionary, or a total of nine hundred and sixty-six, the total converts in China would have numbered well-nigh a million souls, whereas the actual baptisms for that year in China numbered only thirty-eight thousand, seven hundred and twenty-four."

The last Sabbath spent in Toronto was an extremely strenuous one for Dr. Goforth, speaking four times. Weeks later, testimonies came from some of those attending the evening service. All of these referred to the "radiancy" of Dr. Goforth's face as he gave his last message in Toronto.

On October 7, Dr. Goforth's speaking appointment was forty miles distant from our son, Frederic's house, where we were staying. His address that evening was on "How the Spirit's Fire Swept Korea," one of the longest and most testing of his messages. Refreshments were served at the close of the service, but Dr. Goforth declined to partake, saying he had "a little indigestion." It was very late when he finally got to rest that night. About seven o'clock the following morning, I rose and dressed, thinking my husband was still sleeping, but as he remained strangely quiet, I looked more closely and saw that my husband's earthly casket was there, but that _he_ had passed the Borderland into "the land that is fairer than day." His attitude was one of complete rest, his face resting on one hand, relaxed and open, while the other, also relaxed, lay beside it. The doctor said he had passed just about the time I had risen and _had not known death_. He simply slept one moment on earth; the next, he was awake and _seeing once more_ in the Gloryland. He had said but a few weeks before when at "Ben Lippen," that he rejoiced to know the next face he would see would be his Saviour's. "I shall be _satisfied_ when I awake with Thy likeness" (Psalm 17:15).

Those who were present at the funeral service held in Knox Church, Toronto, can never forget the triumphant note which sounded all through the service. Our thoughts were not centered on what lay beyond that great bank of flowers; rather did we all feel Jonathan Goforth's radiant, joyous spirit present with us.

Rev. Dr. John Gibson Inkster, Pastor, Knox Presbyterian Church, Toronto, spoke as follows:

"He was a God-intoxicated man—fully surrendered and consecrated. Above all, he was humble. He was baptized with the Holy Ghost and with fire. He was filled with the Spirit because he was emptied of self— therefore he had power which prevailed with God and man. He knew what it was to pray the prayer of faith in the Holy Ghost."

Rev. James MacKay, who had recently visited Manchuria said:

"Love begets love, and I can testify that wherever we went in Manchuria we saw evidence of the love of the Manchurian people for the Goforths. In fact, so great did we find that love to be, that we regarded it as coming perilously near to worship. They loved him, however, because he first loved them, and showed that love by giving them his all. He greatly loved and he was greatly beloved."